Praise fron

MW01273698

"At first glance I thought that this might be just another book of SAS coding examples. Not so! A closer inspection shows that this book is all about the problems and issues, some big and some small, that are sure to cause heartburn when they are encountered. It provides both standard and nonstandard solutions to a wide variety of production situations. Before you pull your hair out, grab this book…it will save you both time and money."

Art Carpenter
California Occidental Consultants

"Phil Holland's unique, valuable book covers not only fundamental concerns common to all programmers (such as disk space usage and processing run times), but also their potential needs (for example, accessing SAS data without SAS code and transporting data between SAS and databases without using SAS/ACCESS). There is wise advice to enable you to get the most out of your hardware when using SAS. But most remarkable are the creative ideas and ingenious methods of this versatile author, eminently skilled in both SAS and other software, that can help you to get the most out of your existing SAS software by integrating it with other software that you might already have. This book is a resource without equal."

LeRoy Bessler, Ph.D.
SAS User Since 1978

"This book offers an eclectic mix of practical techniques for getting more out of your investment in SAS software. It is rare to find z/OS mainframe, Windows PC, UNIX, and client/server information in the same book, but Phil achieves this feat most effectively.

"His fully worked code examples and detailed explanations should enable readers not only to create their own programs when using these techniques but also to understand how and why their programs work. Use this guide to explore the capabilities of the SAS software you license, and you will surely enhance the value of those assets."

Steve Morton
Principal Consultant
Applied System Knowledge Ltd.

"I've enjoyed reading Phil's book. It has a good mix of text and illustrations, making the book readable and instantly usable. Phil's sound, experienced advice is all very practical, and there's something in the book for everyone from SAS novices to metadata and macro masters. My copy of the book is now well-thumbed and stays within easy reach."

Andrew Ratcliffe
RTSL.eu ("Solutions in SAS")

"I like Phil Holland's new book because it is quick and easy to use. You can dive in and find useful examples of code that you can incorporate immediately to craft your own solutions. With the combination of this functionality and the many step-by-step instructions and screen shots, this book will pay for itself in the amount of time it saves. I also really like the mix of topics and SAS products used, which goes where the topic leads and incorporates everything from SAS Enterprise Guide to DB2, and Base SAS to DB2 on z/OS. I highly recommend this book, which I think will be used by SAS programmers very frequently as they go about their day-to-day programming tasks."

Phil Mason
Independent SAS Consultant and Author

Publishing

Saving Time and Money Using SAS®

Philip R. Holland

The correct bibliographic citation for this manual is as follows: Holland, Philip R. 2007. *Saving Time and Money Using SAS®*. Cary, NC: SAS Institute Inc.

Saving Time and Money Using SAS®

Copyright © 2007, SAS Institute Inc., Cary, NC, USA

ISBN 978-1-59047-574-4

All rights reserved. Produced in the United States of America.

1st printing, June 2007

SAS® Publishing provides a complete selection of books and electronic products to help customers use SAS software to its fullest potential. For more information about our e-books, e-learning products, CDs, and hard-copy books, visit the SAS Publishing Web site at **support.sas.com/pubs** or call 1-800-727-3228.

Contents

Acknowledgments

- My wife, Angela, and my three daughters, Sarah, Rachel, and Jessica, for their tolerance and encouragement.

- Bruce Bovill, formerly of SAS UK, for introducing me to SAS software while we were both working at the University of London Computer Centre.

- Jeremy Rankcom, SAS Australia (formerly of SAS UK), for his advice on SAS Enterprise Guide software.

- LeRoy Bessler, Assurant Health, for his advice on SAS/GRAPH software.

- Keefe Hayes, SAS Institute, for his invaluable assistance in running mainframe SAS with DB2.

- Julie Platt and Donna Faircloth, SAS Publishing, for encouraging and supporting my writing, and the editing and production teams for their work on my final manuscript.

- VIEWS committee members, for giving me the chance to present my ideas at VIEWS conferences and in *VIEWS News*.

x

Introduction

When selecting a technical book for myself I tend to choose one where there are lots of examples and sample code snippets that I can use and adapt for my own development projects. I wanted to write a book that I could use for reference myself, so I have tried to make sure there are code snippets wherever possible.

Instead of licensing additional SAS components at your site, I believe you will continue to use SAS software for longer if you have a deeper knowledge of your existing components. Most of the recently introduced SAS components have functionality that can be provided using your existing components. Introducing new components may save maintenance costs, but at the expense of valuable programming expertise.

As a former performance analyst, I still look at any programs I write to see if I can make them smaller, quicker, and/or easier to maintain. Resources may appear to be limitless, but there will inevitably come a day when a program needs more, e.g., WORK disk space, memory, processing power, faster disk access, etc. Looking at your existing programs will move that day further into the future, saving money on resources and maintenance. I have spent the majority of my time as an independent consultant assisting my clients to make better use of their existing components by demonstrating new features, improving their coding efficiency, and helping them to develop applications that are easier to maintain. I want this book to continue this work.

Some of the chapters look at the way information stored in SAS data sets can be viewed using applications other than SAS, e.g., with the SAS ODBC driver, with SAS Integration Technologies, and with graphical report files from SAS/GRAPH programs.

Other chapters concentrate on techniques to optimize specific tasks, e.g., merging data from SAS data sets and external database tables, and the use of disk space.

The remaining chapters demonstrate how to accomplish a particular task without having to license a new SAS component, e.g., reading data from and writing data to databases and spreadsheets without the need to license SAS/ACCESS software, and developing SAS programs on a PC without having Base SAS software installed there.

During the research I carried out while writing this book I greatly increased my knowledge of SAS. I hope that by reading this book and experimenting with the examples, you can increase your understanding of SAS software too, and that the book will help you to get full value out of the SAS components you are licensing.

The following sections provide brief overviews of the chapters in this book.

Chapter 1: Accessing SAS Data without Using SAS Code (Windows only)

Recent developments in SAS for Windows have provided users with routes to SAS data and applications without having to write SAS code using SAS. This chapter describes three very different interfaces to SAS: ODBC, DDE, and SAS Integration Technologies, which could place SAS at the center of any application development for the Windows platform. I have tried to select a diverse range of applications other than SAS to demonstrate the scope of this integration.

Chapter 2: Out of Space with SAS Software? (z/OS, with Windows and UNIX Examples)

When running SAS programs on a PC, users need to worry only about how much free space there is on the PC they are using. However, when SAS programs are run under z/OS on a mainframe machine, the correct use of disk space for WORK and permanent SAS data libraries is more complex, but essential to their smooth running. This chapter describes various methods of exploiting the space available on a mainframe, but also considers how some of these methods can be applied to other platforms such as Windows and UNIX.

Chapter 3: Why Does My Job Run So Slowly? (z/OS Only)

Almost every operation you are able to perform using SAS software can be achieved in many different ways, each with its own advantages and disadvantages. It is not always possible to predict the disadvantages, as a basic operation may be suitable in one circumstance but may be totally inappropriate in another. Using SAS/ACCESS software and PROC SQL gives you a wide variety of alternative methods but, in general, only one is likely to give a solution and a fast response time. This chapter explores these choices and gives insight into how to determine the most efficient approach. It is not always possible to predict in advance which solution will be the quickest, but I hope my discussion will help you to see, after the event, why any solution is not!

Chapter 4: Distributing SAS/GRAPH Reports (All Platforms)

The early releases of SAS/GRAPH software were used on large mainframe computers, and its device drivers catered almost exclusively to the dot-matrix and pen plotters, or to dumb terminals, which were widely used at the time for graphical reporting. If a graphical report was required to be distributed around a business, it would be stored in a SAS/GRAPH catalog, and a SAS program would be executed to reprint the report whenever it was required.

Now there are more requirements for storing graphical reports in files so that they can be distributed around an organization as individual pictures, or as part of illustrated reports from word processors or on Web pages, as universal access to SAS software installations is no longer as common. This chapter discusses a number of methods of producing portable graphic report formats using SAS/GRAPH, none of which require SAS/GRAPH software to be installed on the recipient's system.

Chapter 5: Importing Data from and Exporting Data to Databases without SAS/ACCESS (All Platforms)

This chapter discusses a number of methods of importing data from and exporting data to external databases and spreadsheets using SAS software without the need to license SAS/ACCESS software. It also looks at techniques for reading specific data types, e.g., EBCDIC characters, packed and zoned decimals, dates and times, etc., from flat files into SAS data sets.

Chapter 6: Developing SAS Applications Using SAS Enterprise Guide (Windows Client)

The bundling of SAS Enterprise Guide with SAS®9 has introduced a much greater number of users to this thin-client front end to SAS. Using a thin client, rather than SAS on a PC, to develop SAS applications requires different techniques to get the best out of the new environment. This chapter discusses a number of features of SAS Enterprise Guide that can assist both novice and experienced SAS developers. It also describes a case study involving the introduction of SAS Enterprise Guide and SAS software to a new client site.

Final Thoughts

It has taken a very long time to write this book. This has, in part, been due to project commitments to my clients, but mostly due to my unwillingness to let an interesting topic go. There are still a number of topics in most of the chapters in this book that have not been fully explored. However, because fully exploring all the interesting topics would have meant never finishing the book, I have reluctantly decided to call time on my writing efforts.

I am sure that you will have questions that are not fully answered, or that are not even covered in this book. Therefore, as I have not been discouraged from writing more, I would welcome comments and suggestions for topics and ideas for a future book, particularly if you enjoy reading this book or, at least, find this book helpful. My hope is that this book will encourage you to continue to use SAS coding to develop your business processes, rather than relying on black box applications.

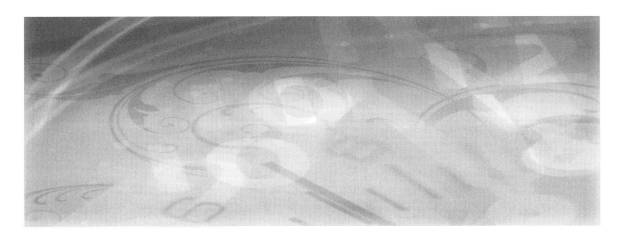

C h a p t e r 1

Accessing SAS Data without Using SAS Code

1.1 Abstract

Recent developments in SAS for Windows have provided users with routes to SAS data and applications without having to write SAS code using SAS. This chapter describes three examples of these interfaces: ODBC, DDE, and SAS Integration Technologies, which could place SAS at the center of any application development for the Windows platform.

1.2 Introduction

In the past, SAS has been used to read data from other Windows data sources, e.g., Microsoft Access tables using SAS/ACCESS for ODBC, and to control other external Windows applications using Dynamic Data Exchange (DDE). SAS is, of course, available as a Windows application itself and can now be used as an external application for those other Windows applications. This role reversal expands the range of uses for SAS in the Windows environment in areas where SAS has not been traditionally the first-choice application. The ability of SAS to read and maintain data from a wide range of sources can now be used throughout the Windows arena.

Further discussion on SAS Enterprise Guide, a thin-client application for the Windows client platform that uses SAS Integration Technologies to communicate with SAS installations on remote servers, can be found in Chapter 6 "Developing SAS Applications Using SAS Enterprise Guide."

1.3 ODBC

The SAS ODBC driver has been supplied with Base SAS for Windows since SAS 6.10 to provide an interface to SAS data libraries for other Windows applications. Each application has its own particular uses and limitations for the ODBC interface. This section describes the practicalities of using the SAS ODBC driver 9.1 with Microsoft

Access 2000, Microsoft Excel 2000, Visual Basic 6.0, Lotus Approach Version 9, and OpenOffice.org 2.1. It should be noted here that StarOffice 8 is functionally equivalent to OpenOffice.org 2.1, and so all future references to OpenOffice.org 2.1 can be assumed to include StarOffice 8.

Single ODBC access to SAS data on the same machine that the user accesses uses the ODBCSERV procedure, which is supplied with Base SAS, running in a single SAS region. Multiple ODBC access to SAS data, or ODBC access to a remote machine, requires SAS/SHARE, and possibly SAS/SHARE*NET as well.

1.3.1 Setting Up a SAS Server for the SAS ODBC Driver

It is very important to plan, in advance, which SAS data libraries will be accessed via the SAS ODBC driver, as the LIBNAME statements must be defined using the ODBC Administrator application by selecting **Start ▶ Control Panel ▶ Administrative Tools ▶ Data Sources (ODBC)**. In particular, for any ODBC data source, there can be only one library reference that can be written to by an external application, i.e., USER, as Microsoft Access and similar applications can write to data sets with a single-level data set name only. This name, say XYZZY, would be assumed to be the data set WORK.XYZZY, except that the USER library name will override the normal default WORK library name, allowing permanent SAS data sets to be created whenever single-level names are used.

Other features of the ODBC data source definitions include the following:

- The SAS ODBC server must be added to the SERVICES file (found in C:\WINDOWS or C:\WINNT\SYSTEM32\DRIVERS\ETC, depending on the Windows platform used) prior to using the ODBC Administrator, as the SAS ODBC driver uses a TCP/IP connection to communicate with the SAS ODBC server. The additional lines should look like the following line, with a unique number greater than 1024 and the columns separated by tab characters:

  ```
  sasuser32     7001/tcp      #SAS OBDC Server
  ```

- Command line options when invoking SAS (e.g., -AUTOEXEC, -NOLOGO, etc.).
- SAS data library names used for importing into external Windows applications.
- Changes to the library references in a running SAS ODBC server can be made for subsequent ODBC connections.
- Library references within SAS 8 are limited to eight characters, which are not case sensitive. The names cannot include blanks or punctuation, must start with an alphabetic or underscore character, and the second and subsequent characters may be numeric characters.

- It should be noted that the SAS ODBC driver is unable to read the supplied SAS library references (i.e., MAPS, SASUSER, and SASHELP) using its own special library references. If these library references need to be read, they should be allocated to different library references in the ODBC Server Libraries panel, e.g., SMAPS, SUSER, and SHELP.

- Finally, but probably the most important, if you are trying to use the SAS ODBC driver on a Windows platform protected by a personal firewall, because the SAS ODBC server is accessed via a TCP/IP port, you will only be able to access the SAS ODBC server port if explicitly permitted by the personal firewall rules.

The setup procedure is as follows:

1. Select a user data sources (driver), e.g., **SAS**.

2. Click **Finish**.

3. Select a data source name, e.g., **SASUSER32**.

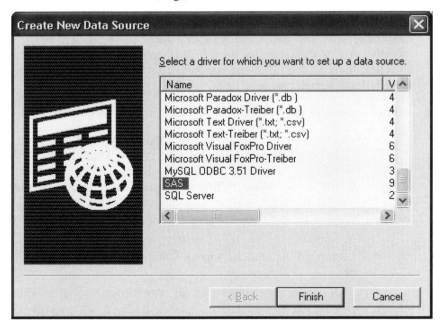

4. Select a description, e.g., **SAS 9.1 ODBC Server**.

5. Select a server, e.g., **sasserv1**.

6. Click the **Servers** tab.

7. Select a server name, e.g., **sasserv1**.

8. Click **Configure**.

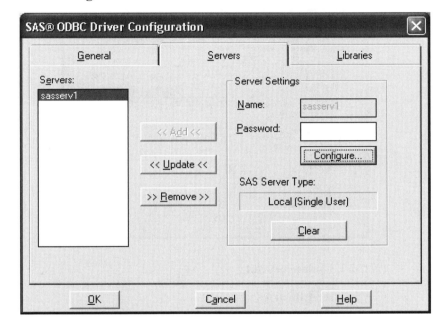

9. Select a SAS path, e.g., **C:\Program Files\SAS\SAS 9.1\sas.exe**. Note that this path can be used to determine which version of SAS is to be used. The SAS ODBC driver 8.2 can support SAS servers of SAS 6, 7, or 8, and the SAS ODBC driver 9.1 can support SAS servers of SAS 7, 8, or 9.

10. Select a SAS parameter, e.g., **-initstmt %sasodbc(sasserv1) -icon -nologo**.

11. Click **OK**.

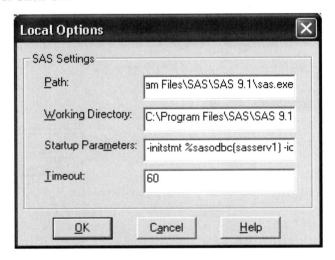

12. Click **Update** or **Add**.

13. Click the **Libraries** tab.

14. Select a library name, e.g., **user**.

15. Select a host file name, e.g., **c:\temp\sas9**.

16. Select a description, e.g., **USER folder**.

17. Click **Add** or **Update**.

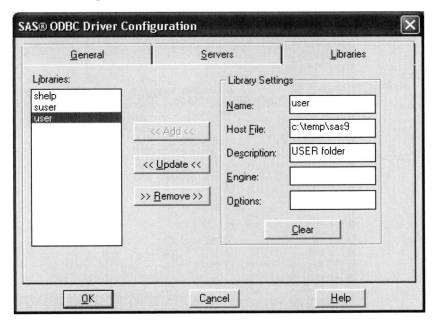

18. Repeat selections as required.

19. Click **OK**.

20. The SAS ODBC driver is now set up for use.

1.3.2 Microsoft Access 2000

Microsoft Access can use the SAS ODBC driver to read from SAS data libraries with the Import menu option, or write to a specific SAS data library with the Export menu option.

The Import procedure is as follows:

1. Select **File ▶ Get External Data ▶ Import**.

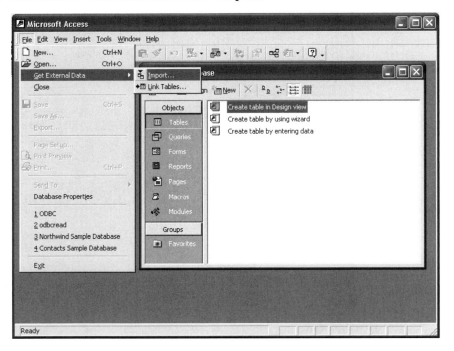

2. Select an import data source, e.g., **ODBC Databases**().

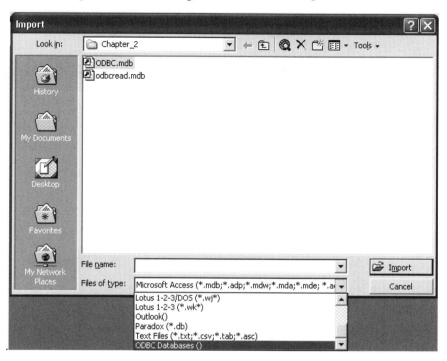

3. Click the **Machine Data Source** tab.

4. Select a data source, e.g., **SASUSER32**.

5. Click **OK**.

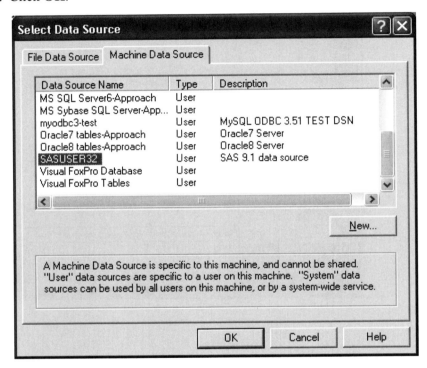

6. Select a data set, e.g., **SHELP_CLASS**.

7. Click **OK**.

8. Data is copied into a new Microsoft Access table, e.g., **SHELP_CLASS**.

Name	Sex	Age	Height	Weight
Alfred	M	14	69	112.5
Alice	F	13	56.5	84
Barbara	F	13	65.3	98
Carol	F	14	62.8	102.5
Henry	M	14	63.5	102.5
James	M	12	57.3	83
Jane	F	12	59.8	84.5
Janet	F	15	62.5	112.5
Jeffrey	M	13	62.5	84
John	M	12	59	99.5
Joyce	F	11	51.3	50.5
Judy	F	14	64.3	90
Louise	F	12	56.3	77
Mary	F	15	66.5	112
Philip	M	16	72	150
Robert	M	12	64.8	128
Ronald	M	15	67	133
Thomas	M	11	57.5	85

Record: 1 of 19

The Export procedure is as follows:

1. Select **File ▶ Export**.

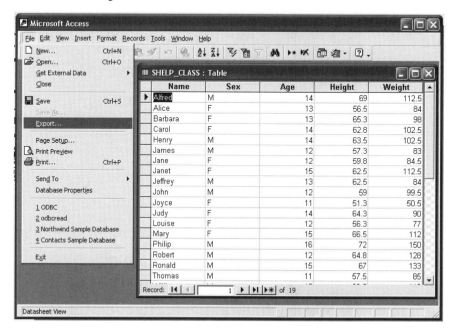

2. Select an export data source, e.g., **ODBC Databases**().

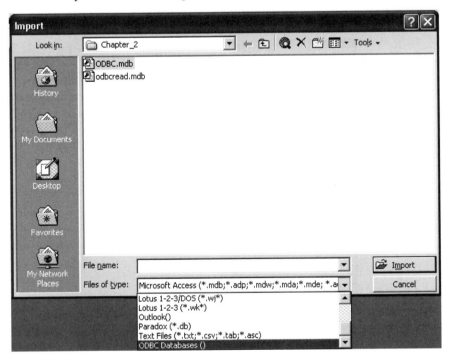

3. Select a Microsoft Access object, e.g., **SHELP_CLASS**.

4. Click **OK**.

5. Click the **Machine Data Source** tab.

6. Select a data source, e.g., **SASUSER32**.

7. Click **OK**.

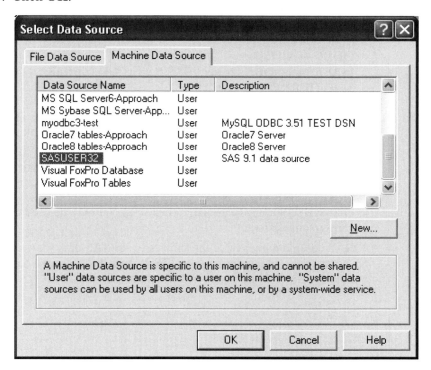

8. Data is copied to a SAS data set, e.g., **USER.SHELP_CLASS**.

Problems

There are several problems when exporting Microsoft Access tables to SAS data libraries:

- Microsoft Access 2000 requires Jet 4.0 with Service Pack 6 applied to export data to a SAS data set. Without the service pack applied, the final step of the preceding export procedure gives the following error message:

  ODBC—call failed.
  [SAS][SAS ODBC Driver][SAS Serve (#-1) [SAS][SAS ODBC Driver][SAS Server]ERROR 76-3 (#-1)

- SAS data sets can only be defined from Microsoft Access as single-level names, so a USER libname must be allocated in the ODBC setup to receive the exported data set.

- SAS data set names can be a maximum of only eight characters. The names cannot include punctuation or blanks. They can include only alphabetic characters (i.e., A–Z or a–z) or underscores as the first and subsequent characters. Numeric characters (i.e., 0–9) can only be used as the second and subsequent characters.

- SAS column names have the same rules as SAS data set names. Microsoft Access has a menu option (i.e., **File ▶ Imp/Exp Setup**) to allow changes to be made to the field information before exporting.

1.3.3 **Microsoft Excel 2000**

Microsoft Excel can only use the SAS ODBC driver to read from SAS data libraries with the **Get External Data** menu option.

The procedure is as follows:

1. Select **Data ▶ Get External Data ▶ New Database Query**.

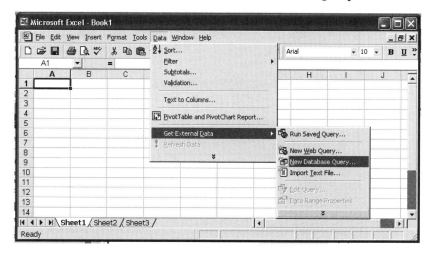

2. Select a data source, e.g., **SASUSER32***.

3. Select the **Use the Query Wizard to create/edit queries** check box.

4. Click **OK**.

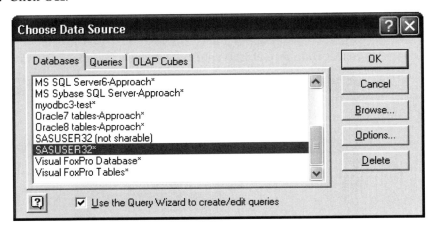

5. Select a data set, e.g., **CLASS**.

6. Click the right arrow (>) to select all the columns in your query. To select a subset of the columns, click the plus sign (+) next to the data set name first.

7. Click **Next**.

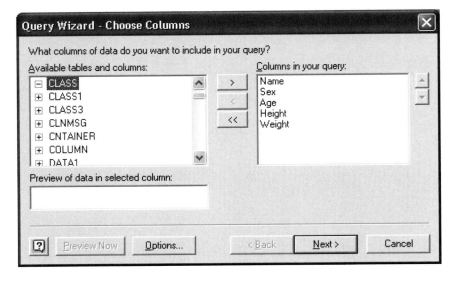

8. Select the columns to filter.

9. Click **Next**.

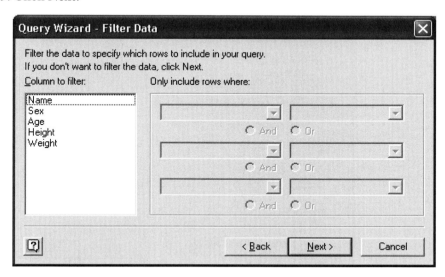

10. Select the sort order.

11. Click **Next**.

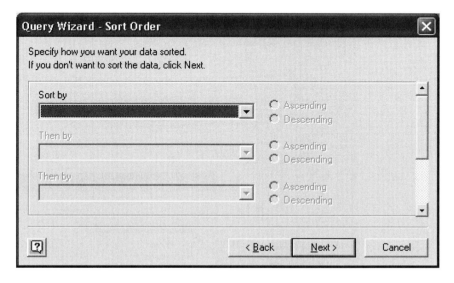

12. Select **Return Data to Microsoft Excel**.

13. Click **Finish**.

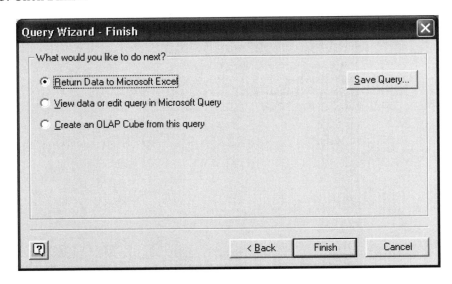

14. Select where you want to put the data.

15. Click **OK**.

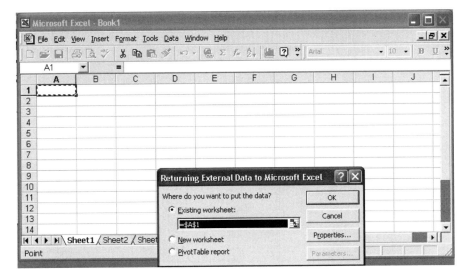

16. Data is inserted at the destination location.

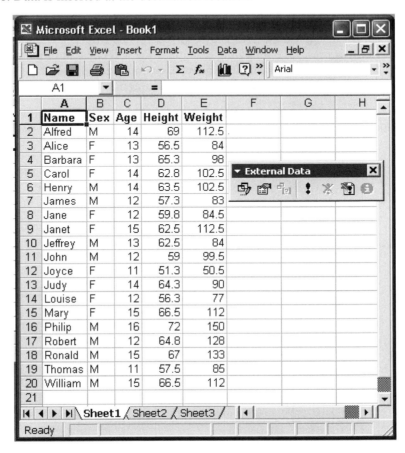

1.3.4 Visual Basic 6.0

Visual Basic can use the SAS ODBC driver to read from SAS data libraries, with shared read-only access. The following example code will copy all of the data from a SAS data set into a dBase table, which can be read, or imported, into all the database and spreadsheet applications discussed in this chapter.

In order to be able to copy the SAS data from the ODBC connection to the dBase table, the target table has to be constructed to include exactly the same fields:

```
Public Function CopyStructDAO(daoRset1 As DAO.Recordset, _
                              daoDB2 As DAO.Database, _
                              DBTable As String) As Integer
   Dim i As Integer
   Dim daoTDef2 As DAO.TableDef
   Dim tmpTDef As DAO.TableDef
   Dim daoFld2 As DAO.Field
   Dim daoFld1 As DAO.Field
   Dim errorFlag As Boolean
   ' Search to see if table exists
   For i = 0 To daoDB2.TableDefs.Count - 1
     Set tmpTDef = daoDB2.TableDefs(i)
     If UCase(tmpTabDef.Name) = UCase(DBTable) Then
       daoDB2.TableDefs.Delete tmpTDef.Name
       Exit For
     End If
   Next
   Set daoTDef2 = daoDB2.CreateTableDef(DBTable)
   ' Strip off owner if present
   daoTDef2.Name = StripOwner(DBTable)
   ' Create fields
   For i = 0 To daoRset1.Fields.Count - 1
     Set daoFld1 = daoRset1.Fields(i)
     Set daoFld2 = Nothing
     errorFlag = True
     Select Case daoFld1.Type
       Case dbDouble
         Set daoFld2 = daoTDef2.CreateField(CVar(daoFld1.Name),_
                                 Cvar(daoFld1.Type))
         errorFlag = False
       Case dbText
         Set daoFld2 = daoTDef2.CreateField(CVar(daoFld1.Name),_
                                 Cvar(daoFld1.Type), _
                                 Cvar(daoFld1.FieldSize))
         errorFlag = False
     End Select
```

```
      If Not errorFlag Then
        daoTDef2.Fields.Append daoFld2
      End If
    Next
    ' Append new table
    daoDB2.TableDefs.Append daoTDef2
    CopyStructDAO = True
End Function
```

Once the table structure has been copied and the two tables opened as recordsets, the data itself can then be copied record by record, 1,000 records at a time, using transactions:

```
Public Function CopyDataDAO(defWSpace As Workspace, _
                            daoRset1 As DAO.Recordset, _
                            daoRset2 As DAO.Recordset) As Integer
    Dim i As Integer
    Dim j As Integer
    Dim numRecords As Integer
    Dim daoFld1 As DAO.Field
    Dim daoFld2 As DAO.Field
    ' Start workspace transactions
    defWSpace.BeginTrans
    While daoRset1.EOF = False
      daoRset2.AddNew
      ' Loop copies data from each field to new table
      For i = 0 To (daoRset1.Fields.Count - 1)
        Set daoFld1 = daoRset1.Fields(i)
        For j = 0 To (daoRset2.Fields.Count - 1)
          Set daoFld2 = daoRset2.Fields(j)
          If UCase(daoFld1.Name) = UCase(daoFld2.Name) Then
            daoRset2(daoFld2.Name).Value = daoFld1.Value
            Exit For
          End If
        Next
      Next
      daoRset2.Update
      daoRset1.MoveNext
      numRecords = numRecords + 1
      ' Commit transactions every 1000 records
      If numRecords = 1000 Then
        defWSpace.CommitTrans
        defWSpace.BeginTrans
        numRecords = 0
      End If
```

```
      Wend
      ' Commit changes now we have finished
      defWSpace.CommitTrans
      CopyDataDAO = True
   End Function
```

The following function is used to remove "owner" information from the ODBC table names, e.g., SHELP.CLASS becomes CLASS:

```
   Public Function StripOwner(TableName As String) As String
      If InStr(TableName, ".") > 0 Then
        TableName = Mid(TableName, _
                        InStr(TableName, ".") + 1, _
                        Len(TableName))
      End If
      StripOwner = TableName
   End Function
```

The functions already described can be brought together to copy the structure and data from the source table to the target table as follows:

```
   Public Sub SaveDAOToDAO(defWSpace As Workspace, _
                           daoRset1 As DAO.Recordset, _
                           daoDB2 As DAO.Database, _
                           DBTable As String)
      Dim daoRset2 As DAO.Recordset
      Dim i As Integer
      If CopyStructDAO(daoRset1, daoDB2, DBTable) Then
        Set daoRset2 = daoDB2.OpenRecordset(DBTable)
        If CopyDataDAO(defWSpace, daoRset1, daoRset2) Then
          daoRset2.Close

          Debug.Print "CopyData to perm completed..."
        End If
      End If
   End Sub
```

All that is left to do is to specify the ODBC server name and the source and target tables:

```
   Public Sub ODBCread()
      ' Create DAO objects
      Dim odbcDB As DAO.Database
      Dim odbcRset As DAO.Recordset
      Dim defWSpace As Workspace
      Dim daoDB As DAO.Database
      Dim odbcServer As String
      Dim DataSet As String
      Dim DBFilePath As String
```

```
  Dim DBTable As String
  Dim defFileSystem As Object
  Dim DBFileObject As Object
  ' Set file and database folder values
  DataSet = "shelp.class"
  odbcServer = "sasuser32"
  DBTable = "class1"
  DBFilePath = "c:\temp"
  ' Verify path
  Set defFileSystem = CreateObject("Scripting.FileSystemObject")
  Set DBFileObject = defFileSystem.GetFolder(DBFilePath)
  ' Get default workspace.
  Set defWSpace = DBEngine.Workspaces(0)
  ' Make sure there isn't already a file with the same name
  ' in the folder.
  If Dir(Trim$(DBFileObject.Path) & _
         "\" & _
         Trim$(DBTable) & ".dbf") <> "" Then
   Kill Trim$(DBFileObject.Path) & "\" & Trim$(DBTable) & ".dbf"
  End If
  ' Open database
  Set daoDB = defWSpace.OpenDatabase(Trim$(DBFileObject.Path), _
                                     False, _
                                     False, _
                                     "dBase IV;")
  ' Set initialization properties
  Set odbcDB = defWSpace.OpenDatabase(odbcServer, _
                                      False, _
                                      True, _
                                      "ODBC;")
  ' Open recordset
  Set odbcRset = odbcDB.OpenRecordset(DataSet)
  Call SaveDAOToDAO(defWSpace, _
                    odbcRset, _
                    daoDB, _
                    DBTable)
  ' Close connection
  odbcRset.Close
  odbcDB.Close
  daoDB.Close
  Set defWSpace = Nothing
End Sub
```

Visual Basic can also use the SAS ODBC driver to write to SAS data libraries, with exclusive update access, using the following DatabaseName and Connect strings, e.g.:

```
Set DB = OpenDatabase("saswrite", True, False, "ODBC;")
```

The database, "DB", can be manipulated in the same way as any Microsoft Access database using standard Visual Basic Data Access functions and methods. The SAS data sets within the ODBC data source can be accessed using the standard SAS 'libref.member' naming conventions, via Jet SQL supplied as part of Visual Basic and Microsoft Access.

1.3.5 Lotus Approach Version 9

LotusScript Version 9

In the same way that Visual Basic can use the SAS ODBC driver to read from SAS data libraries, LotusScript can be used to create a new Approach document to view a SAS data set:

```
Sub ODBCread
  ' Create new connection
  Dim Con As New Connection()
  ' Create new query
  Dim Qry As New Query()
  ' Create new resultset
  Dim RS As New ResultSet()
  Dim MyDoc As Document
  Dim ServName As String
  Dim TName As String
  ' Specify ODBC server name
  ServName = "sasuser32"
  ' Specify source data set name
  TName = "shelp.class"
  ' Open ODBC connection to server
  ' (which must be prefixed with "!")
  If Con.ConnectTo("ODBC Data Sources", , , "!" & ServName) Then
    ' Associate query with connection
    Set Qry.Connection = Con
    ' Set table to open
    Qry.TableName = Tname
    ' Associate resultset with query
    Set RS.Query = Qry
    ' Populate resultset
```

```
    If RS.Execute Then
      ' Create Approach document for resultset
      Set MyDoc = New Document(RS)
    End If
    ' Close connection
    Con.Disconnect
  End If
End Sub
```

1.3.6 OpenOffice.org 2.1

While, in theory, OpenOffice.org Base can use ODBC drivers compatible with ODBC 3 to access database tables, the SAS ODBC driver was compatible only with ODBC 2 prior to SAS 9.1. Following the changes made to the SAS ODBC driver in SAS 9.1, it is now possible to import SAS data into OpenOffice.org spreadsheets without any errors.

Data from a SAS data set can now be imported into OpenOffice.org documents, but it must first be registered in an OpenOffice.org database as follows:

1. Open OpenOffice.org Base.

2. Select **Connect to an existing database**.

3. Select **ODBC** from the drop-down list.

4. Click **Next**.

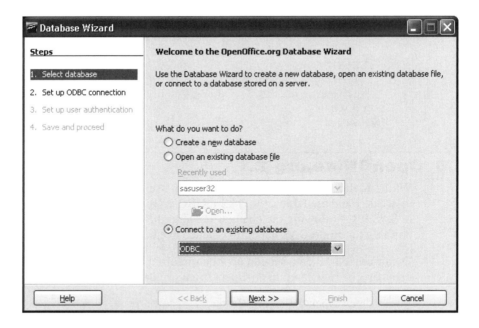

5. Click **Browse**.

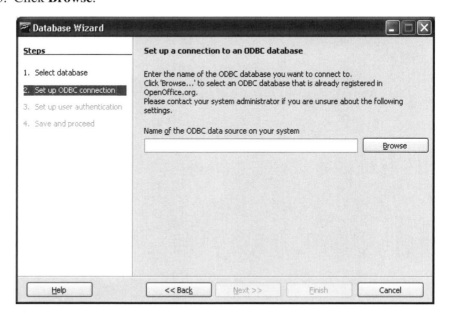

6. Select a data source, e.g., **SASUSER32**.

7. Click **OK**.

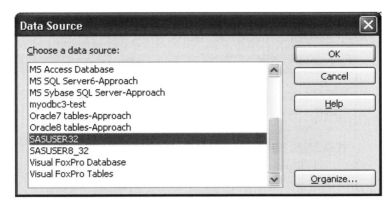

8. Click **Next**.

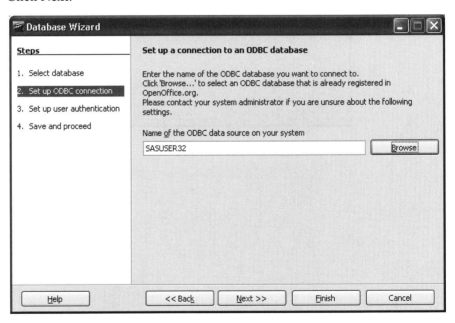

9. If a user name and password are required, fill in the details.

10. The connection to the SAS ODBC data source can be tested by clicking **Test Connection**. Otherwise, click **Next**.

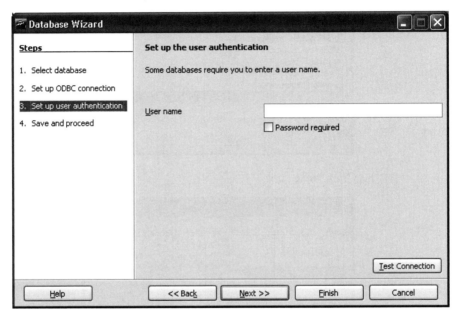

11. Select **Yes, register the database for me**.

12. Click **Finish**.

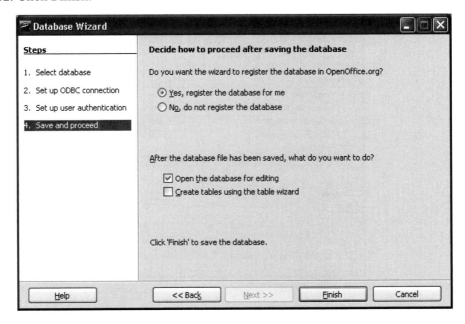

13. Enter the location of the new OpenOffice.org database.

14. Click **Save**.

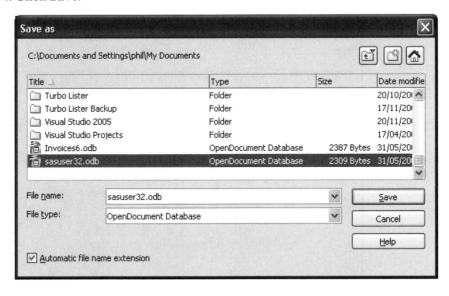

15. The database can now be accessed from an OpenOffice.org document, or reports can be created directly in OpenOffice.org Base.

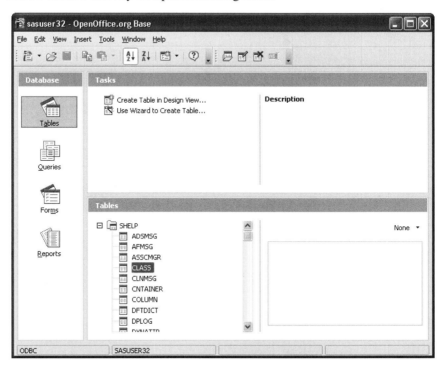

The data from the registered OpenOffice.org database created from the SAS ODBC data source can be added to an OpenOffice.org spreadsheet as follows:

1. Select **Data ▶ DataPilot ▶ Start**.

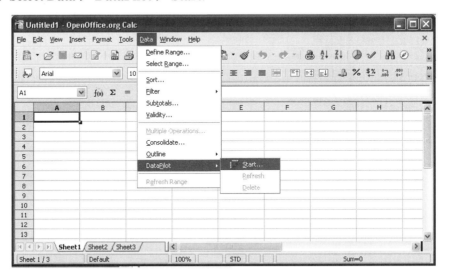

2. Select **Data source registered in OpenOffice.org**.

3. Click **OK**.

4. Select a database from the drop-down list.

5. Select a data source from the drop-down list.

6. Select a type, e.g., **Sheet**.

7. Click **OK**.

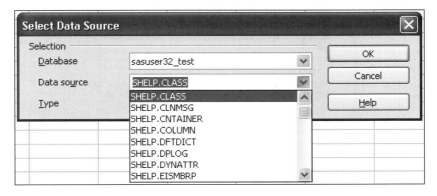

8. Drag fields into the report template.

9. Select a data field, and then click **Options** to change the summary statistic.

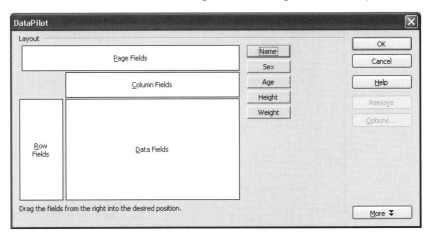

10. Select a statistic from the list for the data field.

11. Click **OK**.

12. Select a column or row field, and then click **Options** to change the subtotals.

13. Select the **Subtotal** option.

14. Click **OK**.

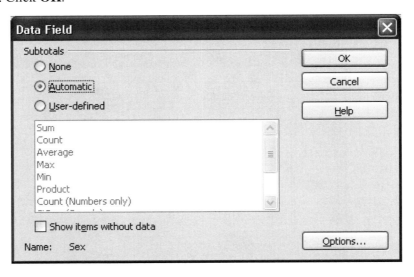

15. Click **OK**.

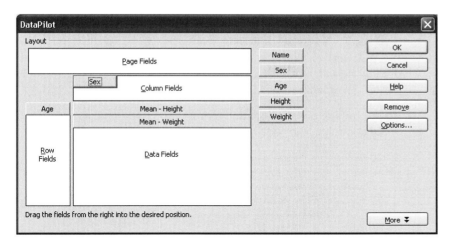

16. The report is generated at the currently selected cell.

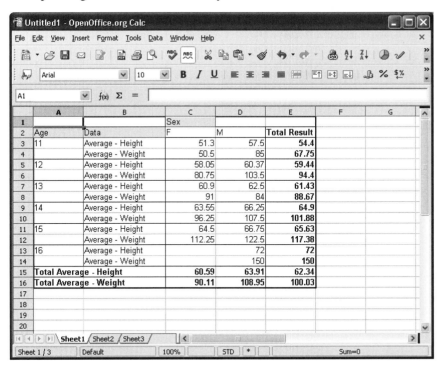

1.3.6.1 Visual Basic 6.0

It is also very easy to use Visual Basic to access the SAS ODBC driver, and then write directly into an OpenOffice.org Calc spreadsheet or into a table in an OpenOffice.org Writer document.

The following code is common to both processes, and should be included before the application-specific code:

```
Dim oServiceManager As Object
Dim oDesktop As Object
' Get the Service Manager object.
Set oServiceManager = _
    CreateObject("com.sun.star.ServiceManager")
' Get the Desktop object.
Set oDesktop = _
  oServiceManager.createInstance("com.sun.star.frame.Desktop")
' Create DAO objects
Dim odbcDB As DAO.Database
Dim odbcRecordset As DAO.Recordset
Dim defWSpace As Workspace
Dim odbcServer As String
Dim DataSet As String
Dim odbcField As Object
' Set file and database folder values
Dim row As Long
Dim column As Long
' Use this empty array when no arguments are needed.
Dim aNoArgs()
DataSet = "shelp.class"
odbcServer = "sasuser32"
' Get default workspace.
Set defWSpace = DBEngine.Workspaces(0)
' Set initialization properties
Set odbcDB = defWSpace.OpenDatabase(odbcServer, _
                                    False, _
                                    True, _
                                    "ODBC;")
' Open recordset
Set odbcRecordset = odbcDB.OpenRecordset(DataSet)
```

The following code is common to both processes, and should be included after the application-specific code:

```
' Close connection
odbcRecordset.Close
odbcDB.Close
Set defWSpace = Nothing
```

OpenOffice.org Calc

```
Dim oCalcDoc As Object
Dim oSheet As Object
' Create a new empty spreadsheet.
Set oCalcDoc = _
  oDesktop.loadComponentFromURL("private:factory/scalc", _
                                "_blank", 0, aNoArgs())
' Get the first spreadsheet from the sheets in the document.
Set oSheet = oCalcDoc.getSheets().getByIndex(0)
' Write table to Calc sheet
'this loop copies each field name into the 1st row of the sheet
row = 0
For column = 0 To (odbcRecordset.Fields.Count - 1)
  Set odbcField = odbcRecordset.Fields(column)
  oSheet.getCellByPosition(column, 0).setFormula _
       CStr(odbcField.Name)
Next
While odbcRecordset.EOF = False
  row = row + 1
  'this loop copies the data from each field to the new table
  For column = 0 To (odbcRecordset.Fields.Count - 1)
    Set odbcField = odbcRecordset.Fields(column)
    If odbcField.Type = 4 or odbcField.Type = 7 Then
      oSheet.getCellByPosition(column, row).setValue _
           odbcField.Value
    Else
      oSheet.getCellByPosition(column, row).setFormula _
           CStr(odbcField.Value)
    End If
  Next
  odbcRecordset.MoveNext
Wend
```

OpenOffice.org Writer

```
Dim oText As Object
Dim oText2 As Object
Dim oTable As Object
Dim oCursor As Object
' Create a new blank text document.
Set oText = _
    oDesktop.loadComponentFromURL("private:factory/swriter", _
                                  "_blank", 0, aNoArgs())
' insert TextTable
Set oTable = _
oText.createInstance("com.sun.star.text.TextTable")
' Create position cursor
Set oText2 = oText.GetText()
Set oCursor = oText2.createTextCursor()
' Write table to Text doc
' initialize the table with the correct number of columns + rows
oTable.Initialize 1, CLng(odbcRecordset.Fields.Count)
oTable.RepeatHeadline = True
' insert table now
oCursor.gotoStart False
oText2.insertTextContent oCursor, oTable, False
'this loop copies each field name into the 1st row of the table
row = 0
For column = 0 To (odbcRecordset.Fields.Count - 1)
  Set odbcField = odbcRecordset.Fields(column)
  oTable.getCellByPosition(column, 0).String = _
      CStr(odbcField.Name)
Next
odbcRecordset.MoveFirst
While odbcRecordset.EOF = False
  row = row + 1
  oTable.GetRows().insertByIndex row, 1
  'this loop copies the data from each field to the new table
  For column = 0 To (odbcRecordset.Fields.Count - 1)
    Set odbcField = odbcRecordset.Fields(column)
    oTable.getCellByPosition(column, row).String = _
        CStr(odbcField.Value)
  Next
  odbcRecordset.MoveNext
Wend
```

1.3.6.2 OpenOffice.org Base 2.1

The Basic programming language within the different components of OpenOffice.org is similar to Visual Basic for Applications. The following Base code, which should be run as a macro within the corresponding component, is functionally the same as the preceding code to access the SAS ODBC driver, and then to write directly into the OpenOffice.org Calc spreadsheet in a sheet called "Class report," or into a new table at the end of the OpenOffice.org Writer document.

The following code is common to both processes, and should be included before the application-specific code:

```
Dim DatabaseContext As Object
Dim DataSource As Object
Dim Connection As Object
Dim InteractionHandler as Object
Dim Statement As Object
Dim ResultSet As Object
Dim row As Long
Dim column As Long
DatabaseContext =
     createUnoService("com.sun.star.sdb.DatabaseContext")
DataSource = DatabaseContext.getByName("sasuser32")
If Not DataSource.IsPasswordRequired Then
  Connection = DataSource.GetConnection("","")
Else
  InteractionHandler =
       createUnoService("com.sun.star.sdb.InteractionHandler")
  Connection =
       DataSource.ConnectWithCompletion(InteractionHandler)
End If
Statement = Connection.createStatement()
ResultSet = Statement.executeQuery("SELECT * FROM shelp.class")
```

The following code is common to both processes, and should be included after the application-specific code:

```
' Close connection
ResultSet.Close
Connection.Close
```

OpenOffice.org Calc

```
Dim Doc As Object
Dim Sheet As Object
Dim Cell As Object
' Create a new empty spreadsheet.
Doc = ThisComponent 'StarDesktop.CurrentComponent
Sheet = Doc.Sheets(0)
If Doc.Sheets.hasByName("Class Report") Then
  Sheet = Doc.Sheets.getByName("Class Report")
Else
  Sheet = Doc.createInstance("com.sun.star.sheet.Spreadsheet")
  Doc.Sheets.insertByName("Class Report", Sheet)
End If
' Write table to Calc sheet
'this loop copies each field name into the 1st row of the sheet
row = 0
For column = 0 To (ResultSet.Columns.Count - 1)
  Cell = Sheet.getCellByPosition(column, 0)
  Cell.Formula = ResultSet.Columns(column).Name
Next
While ResultSet.Next()
  row = row + 1
  'this loop copies the data from each field to the new table
  For column = 0 To (ResultSet.Columns.Count - 1)
    Cell = Sheet.getCellByPosition(column, row)
    If ResultSet.Columns(column).Type = 4 or
       ResultSet.Columns(column).Type = 7 Then
      Cell.Value = ResultSet.Columns(column).getValue()
    Else
      Cell.Formula = ResultSet.Columns(column).getString()
    End If
  Next
Wend
```

OpenOffice.org Writer

```
Dim Doc As Object
Dim Table As Object
Dim Cursor As Object
' Allocate this text document.
Doc = ThisComponent
' Create position cursor
Cursor = Doc.Text.createTextCursor()
' insert table at the end of the document
Cursor.gotoEnd(false)
' insert TextTable
Table = Doc.createInstance("com.sun.star.text.TextTable")
' initialize the table with the correct number of columns + rows
Table.initialize(1, ResultSet.Columns.Count)
' Write table to Text doc
Table.RepeatHeadline = True
Doc.Text.insertTextContent(Cursor, Table, False)
'this loop copies each field name into the 1st row of the table
row = 0
For column = 0 To (ResultSet.Columns.Count - 1)
  Table.getCellByPosition(column, 0)
       .setString(ResultSet.Columns(column).Name)
Next
Table.getRows(0)
While ResultSet.Next()
  row = row + 1
  Table.getRows().insertByIndex(row, 1)
  'this loop copies the data from each field to the new table
  For column = 0 To (ResultSet.Columns.Count - 1)
    Table.getCellByPosition(column, row)
         .setString(ResultSet.Columns(column).getString())
  Next
Wend
```

1.4 Dynamic Data Exchange

In the same way that SAS can be used to start and access Windows applications, SAS can be accessed by other Windows applications using Dynamic Data Exchange (DDE) operations. The DDE interface allows data to be sent to SAS via code (e.g., %LET statements, DATA step code with instream data, etc.). It is possible for SAS Display Manager commands to be executed, menu items to be clicked, SAS code to be written into the Program Editor—in fact any SAS operations that can be performed using the keyboard—using SendKeys instructions that include special string values for special keys, e.g., ALT, CTRL, ESC, ENTER, F1, etc.

Data cannot easily be passed back to the calling program via DDE, but data can be written to a file that can be read by the calling application using SAS code, e.g., as a Microsoft Access table using SAS/ACCESS for ODBC, as comma-separated text to a text file, or as a computer graphics metafile (e.g., *.CGM, *.WMF) using SAS/GRAPH, etc.

Figure 1.1 An Example of a SAS DDE Server at the Center of a Reporting System

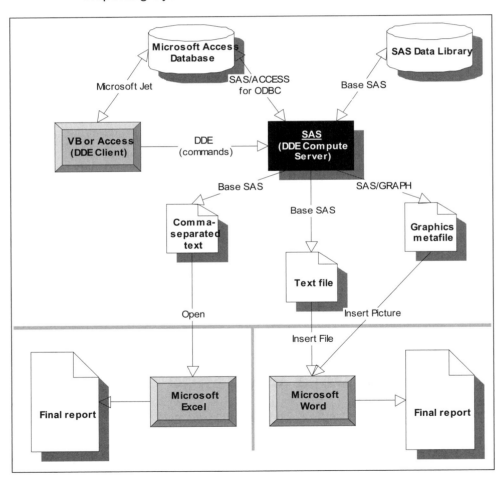

1.4.1 Visual Basic 6.0

Visual Basic 6.0 allows any Visual Basic application to start SAS using a Windows Shell function. When the SAS session has been initialized, commands can be sent to SAS using the SendKeys function, e.g.:

```
'start SAS in maximized window
rc = Shell("d:\sas.exe",vbMaximizedFocus)
'wait for SAS to initialize
For i = 1 To 1000
  DoEvents()
Next
'Globals, Program Editor
SendKeys "%GP",True
'set SAS macro variable
SendKeys "{%}let macrovar = 1234;~",True
'run AF application
SendKeys "dm 'af c=lib.cat.prog.frame' af;~",True
'Locals, Submit
SendKeys "%LS"
'Globals, Program Editor
SendKeys "%GP",True
'Exit SAS
SendKeys "endsas;~",True
'Locals, Submit
SendKeys "%LS"
```

Additional processing by the Visual Basic application would be required if the SAS part of the application allows user input. The Visual Basic application must be hidden from view while the SAS part is executing. One way of performing this is to have a regularly executed function that initially creates a temporary "lock" file, and then hides the Visual Basic window while this file exists. The SAS part can then be seen and run as required. When the SAS processing has been completed, SAS can delete the lock file to tell Visual Basic to restore the visibility of the calling window.

1.5 SAS Integration Technologies

SAS Integration Technologies provides a number of useful external interfaces to SAS data, including an OLE DB driver, which can be accessed using ActiveX Data Objects (ADO), and a SAS Workspace Manager, which provides facilities to execute SAS code. It should be noted that, while access to SAS data via a remote SAS system requires that the SAS Integration Technologies component be licensed on that remote system, access to a local SAS system only requires the installation and licensing of Base SAS.

1.5.1 Visual Basic 6.0

Although the two types of libraries required to access the facilities within SAS Integration Technologies, SAS Integrated Object Model (IOM) and SAS Workspace Manager, are installed at the same time as the client software, they must still be added to the references within your Visual Basic project using the References menu item.

Access to SAS data sets via the OLE DB driver using ADO is very similar to accessing them via the SAS ODBC driver using Data Access Objects (DAO). However, ADO and DAO are not completely interchangeable, e.g., the field attributes are not the same for corresponding data types, which means that the code below has a number of significant differences from that used to access the SAS data sets via ODBC and DAO.

OLE DB and ADO

Allowing for the fact that the data type codes for ADO and DAO are different, and the field attributes also have different names, in order to be able to copy the SAS data from the ADO connection to the dBase table, the target table has to be constructed to include the same fields:

```
Public Function CopyStructADO(adoRset As ADODB.Recordset, _
                              daoDB As DAO.Database, _
                              DBTable As String) As Integer
  Dim i As Integer
  Dim daoTDef As DAO.TableDef
  Dim tmpTDef As DAO.TableDef
  Dim daoFld As DAO.Field
  Dim adoFld As ADODB.Field
  Dim errorFlag As Boolean
  ' Search to see if table exists
  For i = 0 To daoDB.TableDefs.Count - 1
    Set tmpTDef = daoDB.TableDefs(i)
    If UCase(tmpTDef.Name) = UCase(DBTable) Then
      daoDB.TableDefs.Delete tmpTDef.Name
      Exit For
    End If
  Next
  Set daoTDef = daoDB.CreateTableDef(DBTable)
  ' Create fields
  For i = 0 To adoRset.Fields.Count - 1
    Set adoFld = adoRset.Fields(i)
    Set daoFld = Nothing
    errorFlag = True
    ' Convert ADO field types to DAO equivalents
```

```
      Select Case adoFld.Type
        Case adDouble
          Set daoFld = daoTDef.CreateField(CVar(adoFld.Name), _
                                      Cvar(dbDouble))
          errorFlag = False
        Case adChar
          Set daoFld = daoTDef.CreateField(CVar(adoFld.Name), _
                                      Cvar(dbText), _
                                      Cvar(adoFld.DefinedSize))
          errorFlag = False
      End Select
      If Not errorFlag Then
        daoTDef.Fields.Append daoFld
      End If
    Next
    ' Append new table
    daoDB.TableDefs.Append daoTDef
    CopyStructADO = True
End Function
```

Once the table structure has been copied and the two tables opened as recordsets, the data
itself can then be copied record by record, 1,000 records at a time, using transactions:

```
Public Function CopyDataADO(defWSpace As Workspace, _
                              adoRset As ADODB.Recordset, _
                              daoRset As DAO.Recordset) As Integer
    Dim i As Integer
    Dim j As Integer
    Dim numRecords As Integer
    Dim adoFld As ADODB.Field
    Dim daoFld As DAO.Field
    ' Start workspace transactions
    defWSpace.BeginTrans
    While adoRset.EOF = False
      daoRset.AddNew
      ' Loop copies data from each field to new table
      For i = 0 To (adoRset.Fields.Count - 1)
        Set adoFld = adoRset.Fields(i)
        For j = 0 To (daoRset.Fields.Count - 1)
          Set daoFld = daoRset.Fields(j)
          If UCase(adoFld.Name) = UCase(daoFld.Name) Then
            daoRset(daoFld.Name).Value = adoFld.Value
            Exit For
          End If
        Next
      Next
      daoRset.Update
```

```
      adoRset.MoveNext
      numRecords = numRecords + 1
      ' Commit transactions every 1000 records
      If numRecords = 1000 Then
        defWSpace.CommitTrans
        defWSpace.BeginTrans
        numRecords = 0
      End If
   Wend
   ' Commit changes now we have finished
   defWSpace.CommitTrans
   CopyDataADO = True
End Function
```

The functions already described can be brought together to copy the structure and data from the source table to the target table as follows:

```
Public Sub SaveADOToDAO(defWSpace As Workspace, _
                        adoRset As ADODB.Recordset, _
                        daoDB As DAO.Database, _
                        DBTable As String)
   Dim daoRset As DAO.Recordset
   Dim i As Integer
   If CopyStructADO(adoRset, daoDB, DBTable) Then
      Set daoRset = daoDB.OpenRecordset(DBTable)
      If CopyDataADO(defWSpace, adoRset, daoRset) Then
        daoRset.Close
      End If
   End If
End Sub
```

All that is left to do is to specify the location of the SAS data library and the source and target tables:

```
Public Sub ADOread()
   ' Create ADO and DAO objects
   Dim adoConnection As New ADODB.Connection
   Dim adoRset As New ADODB.Recordset
   Dim defWSpace As Workspace
   Dim daoDB As DAO.Database
   Dim FilePath As String
   Dim DataSet As String
   Dim DBFilePath As String
   Dim DBTable As String
   Dim defFileSystem As Object
   Dim adoFileObject As Object
   Dim DBFileObject As Object
```

```
' Set file and database folder values
DataSet = "hello"
FilePath = "c:\temp"
DBTable = "hello1"
DBFilePath = "c:\temp"
' Verify path
Set defFileSystem = CreateObject("Scripting.FileSystemObject")
Set adoFileObject = defFileSystem.GetFolder(FilePath)
Set DBFileObject = defFileSystem.GetFolder(DBFilePath)
' Get default workspace.
Set defWSpace = DBEngine.Workspaces(0)
' Make sure there isn't already a file with the same name
' in the folder.
If Dir(Trim$(DBFileObject.Path) & _
        "\" & _
        Trim$(DBTable) & ".dbf") <> "" Then
    Kill Trim$(DBFileObject.Path) & "\" & Trim$(DBTable) & ".dbf"
End If
' Open database
Set daoDB = defWSpace.OpenDatabase(Trim$(DBFileObject.Path), _
                                    False, _
                                    False, _
                                    "dBase IV;")
' Set initialization properties
adoConnection.Provider = "SAS.LocalProvider.1"
adoConnection.Properties("Data Source") = adoFileObject.Path
' Open connection
adoConnection.Open
' Open recordset
adoRset.Open DataSet, _
             adoConnection, _
             adOpenForwardOnly, _
             adLockReadOnly, _
             adCmdTableDirect
Call SaveADOToDAO(defWSpace, _
                  adoRset, _
                  daoDB, _
                  DBTable)
' Close connection
adoConnection.Close
Set adoConnection = Nothing
daoDB.Close
Set defWSpace = Nothing
End Sub
```

SAS Workspace Manager

The SAS Workspace Manager provides a number of objects that can be used to access the processing power of SAS. In the following examples, SAS will be installed on the same system as the Visual Basic application, thereby not requiring any additional SAS component licensing.

The first example demonstrates how to run a simple SAS program in a local SAS session by submitting code stored in a string array. The SAS.LanguageService object is used to submit the code. The SAS output from the execution of these code lines is written to a text file located in the same folder as the Visual Basic application:

```
Public Sub Wsrun()
  ' Create workspace on local machine using Workspace Manager
  Dim sasWSMgr As New SASWorkspaceManager.WorkspaceManager
  Dim sasWSpace As SAS.Workspace
  Dim errorString As String
  Set sasWSpace = sasWSMgr.Workspaces.CreateWorkspaceByServer _
                    ("My workspace", _
                     VisibilityNone, _
                     Nothing, _
                     "", _
                     "", _
                     errorString)
  Dim sasLangService As SAS.LanguageService
  ' Declare fixed size array of strings to hold input statements
  Dim arraySource(2) As String
  ' Declare dynamic array of strings to hold list output
  Dim arrayList() As String
  ' These arrays will return line types and carriage control
  Dim arrayCC() As LanguageServiceCarriageControl
  Dim arrayLT() As LanguageServiceLineType
  Dim vOutLine As Variant
  arraySource(0) = _
          "data loop; do x=1 to 10; y=2-x; output; end; run;"
  arraySource(1) = "proc print; title 'Loop code';"
  arraySource(2) = "run;"
  Set sasLangService = sasWSpace.LanguageService
  sasLangService.SubmitLines arraySource
  ' Get up to 1000 lines of output
  sasLangService.FlushListLines 1000, arrayCC, arrayLT, arrayList
  ' Print each name in returned array
  Open ".\loop.txt" For Output As #1
  For Each vOutLine In arrayList
    Print #1, vOutLine
```

```
      Next
      Close #1
      sasWSpace.Close
End Sub
```

The second example demonstrates how to use the SAS.DataService object to query the environment of the SAS session to find information about which SAS library references exist. The SAS output from the investigation is written to a text file located in the same folder as the Visual Basic application:

```
Public Sub WSlibname()
    ' Create workspace on local machine using Workspace Manager
    Dim sasWSMgr As New SASWorkspaceManager.WorkspaceManager
    Dim sasWSpace As SAS.Workspace
    Dim errorString As String
    Dim vName As Variant
    ' Declare dynamic array of strings to hold libnames
    Dim arrayLibnames() As String
    Set sasWSpace = sasWSMgr.Workspaces.CreateWorkspaceByServer _
                        ("My workspace", _
                        VisibilityNone, _
                        Nothing, _
                        "", _
                        "", _
                        errorString)
    ' Get reference to workspace's DataService.
    Dim sasDService As SAS.DataService
    Set sasDService = sasWSpace.DataService
    ' Assign libref named "saslib2" within new workspace
    Dim sasLibref As SAS.Libref
    Set sasLibref = sasDService.AssignLibref _
                        ("saslib2", _
                        "", _
                        ".\", _
                        "")
    ' Should print "saslib2"
    Open ".\libref.log" For Output As #2
    Print #2, "Newest libname = " & sasLibref.Name
    Print #2, " "
    ' Pass dynamic array variable to "ListLibrefs".
    ' Upon return, array variable will be filled in with array
    ' of strings one element for each libref in workspace
    sasDService.ListLibrefs arrayLibnames
    ' Print each name in returned array
    For Each vName In arrayLibnames
        Print #2, vName
    Next
```

```
' Print size of array
Print #2, " "
Print #2, "Number of librefs was: " & UBound(arrayLibnames) + 1
Close #2
' Deassign libref.
sasDService.DeassignLibref sasLibref.Name
' Close workspace.
sasWSpace.Close
End Sub
```

SAS Workspace Manager, IOM, and ADO

The SAS Workspace Manager also provides an interface suitable for accessing SAS data sets via ADO. As was seen in the preceding example for the SAS Workspace Manager, the SAS.LanguageService object is used to submit some SAS code to create a temporary SAS data set. The ADO interface then uses the local SAS IOM data provider, SAS.IOMProvider.1, to access the temporary SAS data set. The code then calls the SaveADOToDAO subroutine, described earlier in the section about OLE DB and ADO, to copy its structure and contents to a dBase file:

```
Public Sub WSADOread()
    ' Create workspace on local machine using Workspace Manager
    Dim sasWSpace As SAS.Workspace
    Dim sasWSMgr As New SASWorkspaceManager.WorkspaceManager
    Dim errorString As String
    ' Create ADO and DAO objects
    Dim adoConnection As New ADODB.Connection
    Dim adoRset As New ADODB.Recordset
    Dim defWSpace As Workspace
    Dim daoDB As DAO.Database
    Dim daoRset As DAO.Recordset
    Dim DBFilePath As String
    Dim DBTable As String
    Dim defFileSystem As Object
    Dim DBFileObject As Object
    ' Set file and database folder values
    DBTable = "looping"
    DBFilePath = "c:\temp"
    ' Verify path
    Set defFileSystem = CreateObject("Scripting.FileSystemObject")
    Set DBFileObject = defFileSystem.GetFolder(DBFilePath)
    ' Get default workspace.
    Set defWSpace = DBEngine.Workspaces(0)
    ' Make sure there isn't already a file with the same name
    ' in the folder.
    If Dir(Trim$(DBFileObject.Path) & _
            "\" & _
            Trim$(DBTable) & ".dbf") <> "" Then
```

```
        Kill Trim$(DBFileObject.Path) & "\" & Trim$(DBTable) & ".dbf"
    End If
    ' Open database
    Set daoDB = defWSpace.OpenDatabase(Trim$(DBFileObject.Path), _
                                    True, _
                                    False, _
                                    "dBase IV;")
    Set sasWSpace = sasWSMgr.Workspaces.CreateWorkspaceByServer _
                        ("MyWorkspaceName", _
                        VisibilityProcess, _
                        Nothing, _
                        "", _
                        "", _
                        errorString)
    ' Submit SAS code
    sasWSpace.LanguageService.Submit _
        "data looping; do x=1 to 50; y=100; z=x*x; output; run;"
    ' Connect to local SAS IOM data provider
    adoConnection.Open _
        "Provider=SAS.IOMProvider.1; SAS Workspace ID=" + _
        sasWSpace.UniqueIdentifier
        ' Read temporary SAS data set
    adoRset.Open "work.looping", _
                adoConnection, _
                adOpenStatic, _
                adLockReadOnly, _
                adCmdTableDirect
    ' Copy the data to dBase file
    Call SaveADOToDAO(defWSpace, _
                    adoRset, _
                    daoDB, _
                    DBTable)
    ' Close connections
    adoConnection.Close
    Set adoConnection = Nothing
    daoDB.Close
    Set defWSpace = Nothing
    ' If we don't close SAS, the SAS process may stay around
    ' forever
    If Not (sasWSpace Is Nothing) Then
        sasWSMgr.Workspaces.RemoveWorkspace sasWSpace
        sasWSpace.Close
    End If
End Sub
```

1.5.2 LotusScript Version 9

Lotus Word Pro 9 with SAS Workspace Manager, IOM, and ADO

The SAS Workspace Manager also provides an interface suitable for accessing SAS data sets via ADO, which can also be used within the applications that form Lotus SmartSuite. The following code extracts the data from a SAS data set called CLASS, which is located in the folder **'c:\temp\sas'** (note that the file separators need to be changed in the code to UNIX-style separators!), and then writes it record by record to the end of a Lotus Word Pro document.

```
Sub ADORead_WP()
  Dim vConn As Variant
  ' create connect and recordset options
  Set vConn = CreateObject("ADODB.Connection")
  Set rs = CreateObject("ADODB.recordset")
  ' open the connection to the mdb
  vConn.Provider = "SAS.LocalProvider.1"
  vConn.Open "c:/temp/sas"
  rs.Open "class", vConn, 0, 1, 512
  ' Write the data to the end of the current document.
  .Type "[ctrlEnd]"
  iNumField = rs.Fields.Count
  .Type "[ENTER]Num Fields is " & Str(iNumField) & "[ENTER]"
  rs.MoveFirst
  Do While Not rs.EOF
    .Type "[ENTER]" & rs.Fields("Name").Value
    .Type "[TAB]" & rs.Fields("Age").Value
    .Type "[TAB]" & rs.Fields("Sex").value
    .Type "[TAB]" & rs.Fields("Height").Value
    .Type "[TAB]" & rs.Fields("Weight").Value
    rs.MoveNext
  Loop
  rs.close
  vConn.Close
  Set rs = Nothing
  Set vConn = Nothing
End Sub
```

Lotus 1-2-3 9 with SAS Workspace Manager, IOM, and ADO

The following code performs the same actions as above, but writes the data to cells starting at the top left cell of the first sheet in a Lotus 1-2-3 spreadsheet file. Again, the location of the input SAS data set must be specified in the code with file separators changed to be UNIX-style.

```
Sub ADORead_123()
  Dim vConn As Variant
  Dim row As Long
  Dim report As Range
  Set report = [A:A3..A:E65535]
  ' create connect and recordset options
  Set vConn = CreateObject("ADODB.Connection")
  Set rs = CreateObject("ADODB.recordset")
  ' open the connection to the mdb
  vConn.Provider = "SAS.LocalProvider.1"
  vConn.Open "c:/temp/sas"
  rs.Open "class", vConn, 0, 1, 512
  iNumField = rs.Fields.Count
  [A:A1].Contents = "Num Fields is " & Str(iNumField)
  [A:A2].Contents = "Name"
  [A:B2].Contents = "Age"
  [A:C2].Contents = "Sex"
  [A:D2].Contents = "Height"
  [A:E2].Contents = "Weight"
  rs.MoveFirst
  row = 0
  Do While Not rs.EOF
    report.Cell(row,0).Contents = rs.Fields("Name").Value
    report.Cell(row,1).Contents = rs.Fields("Age").Value
    report.Cell(row,2).Contents = rs.Fields("Sex").Value
    report.Cell(row,3).Contents = rs.Fields("Height").Value
    report.Cell(row,4).Contents = rs.Fields("Weight").Value
    rs.MoveNext
    row = row + 1
  Loop
  rs.close
  vConn.Close
  Set rs = Nothing
  Set vConn = Nothing
End Sub
```

1.5.3 OpenOffice.org 2.1

It is easier to use Visual Basic to access the SAS Integration Technologies services, and then write directly into an OpenOffice.org Calc spreadsheet or into a table in an OpenOffice.org Writer document.

The following code is common to both processes, and should be included before the application-specific code:

```
Dim oServiceManager As Object
Dim oDesktop As Object
' Get the Service Manager object.
Set oServiceManager = _
    CreateObject("com.sun.star.ServiceManager")
' Get the Desktop object.
Set oDesktop = _
    oServiceManager.createInstance("com.sun.star.frame.Desktop")
Dim adoConnection As New ADODB.Connection
Dim adoRecordset As New ADODB.Recordset
Dim FilePath As String
Dim DataSet As String
Dim defFileSystem As Object
Dim adoFileObject As Object
Dim adoField As Object
Dim row As Long
Dim column As Long
' Use this empty array when no arguments are needed.
Dim aNoArgs()
' Set file values
FilePath = "c:\temp\sas"
DataSet = "class"
' Verify path
Set defFileSystem = CreateObject("Scripting.FileSystemObject")
Set adoFileObject = defFileSystem.GetFolder(FilePath)
' Set initialization properties
adoConnection.Provider = "SAS.LocalProvider.1"
adoConnection.Properties("Data Source") = adoFileObject.Path
' Open the Connection and display its properties
adoConnection.Open
' Open the Recordset
adoRecordset.Open DataSet, _
                  adoConnection, _
                  adOpenForwardOnly, _
                  adLockReadOnly, _
                  ADODB.adCmdTableDirect
```

The following code is common to both processes, and should be included after the application-specific code:

```
' Close the Connection
adoConnection.Close
Set adoConnection = Nothing
```

OpenOffice.org Calc

```
Dim oCalcDoc As Object
Dim oSheet As Object
' Create a new empty spreadsheet.
Set oCalcDoc = _
    oDesktop.loadComponentFromURL("private:factory/scalc", _
                                  "_blank", 0, aNoArgs())
' Get the first spreadsheet from the sheets in the document.
Set oSheet = oCalcDoc.getSheets().getByIndex(0)
' Write table to Calc sheet
'this loop copies each field name into the 1st row of the sheet
row = 0
For column = 0 To (adoRecordset.Fields.Count - 1)
    Set adoField = adoRecordset.Fields(column)
    oSheet.getCellByPosition(column, 0).setFormula _
        CStr(adoField.Name)
Next
While adoRecordset.EOF = False
    row = row + 1
    'this loop copies the data from each field to the new table
    For column = 0 To (adoRecordset.Fields.Count - 1)
        Set adoField = adoRecordset.Fields(column)
        If adoField.Type = 200 Then
            oSheet.getCellByPosition(column, row).setFormula _
                CStr(adoField.Value)
        Else
            oSheet.getCellByPosition(column, row).setValue _
                adoField.Value
        End If
    Next
    adoRecordset.MoveNext
Wend
```

OpenOffice.org Writer

```
Dim oText As Object
Dim oText2 As Object
Dim oTable As Object
Dim oCursor As Object
' Create a new blank text document.
Set oText = _
        oDesktop.loadComponentFromURL("private:factory/swriter", _
                                      "_blank", 0, aNoArgs())
' insert TextTable
Set oTable = oText.createInstance("com.sun.star.text.TextTable")
' Create position cursor
Set oText2 = oText.GetText()
Set oCursor = oText2.createTextCursor()
' Write table to Text doc
' initialize the table with the correct number of columns + rows
oTable.Initialize 1, CLng(adoRecordset.Fields.Count)
oTable.RepeatHeadline = True
' insert table now
oCursor.gotoStart False
oText2.insertTextContent oCursor, oTable, False
'this loop copies each field name into the 1st row of the table
row = 0
For column = 0 To (adoRecordset.Fields.Count - 1)
    Set adoField = adoRecordset.Fields(column)
    oTable.getCellByPosition(column, 0).String = _
            CStr(adoField.Name)
Next
adoRecordset.MoveFirst
While adoRecordset.EOF = False
    row = row + 1
    oTable.GetRows().insertByIndex row, 1
    'this loop copies the data from each field to the new table
    For column = 0 To (adoRecordset.Fields.Count - 1)
        Set adoField = adoRecordset.Fields(column)
        oTable.getCellByPosition(column, row).String = _
                CStr(adoField.Value)
    Next
    adoRecordset.MoveNext
Wend
```

1.6 Conclusions

This chapter has only scraped the surface of what is possible using SAS as a file server or compute server for other Windows-based applications. It should now be clear that a large number of different PC users could benefit from using SAS effectively as a "black box" processor with their own applications, reducing the need to fully train them in SAS coding techniques. The SAS data libraries and SAS application development can be done for them by SAS specialists, providing the users with a well-documented and stable interface that they can use without any requirement for prior knowledge of SAS.

1.7 Recommended Reading

For more information, go to www.hollandnumerics.com/books/Saving_Time_and_Money_using_SAS.htm. This page includes a chapter-by-chapter list of recommended reading.

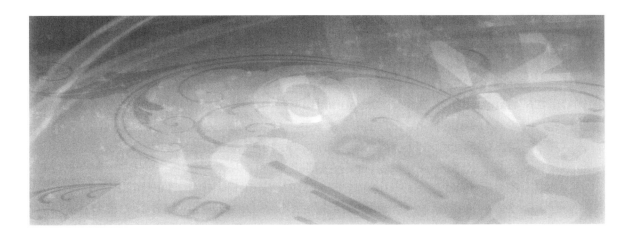

Chapter 2

Out of Space with SAS Software?

2.1 Abstract

When running SAS programs on a PC, users need to worry only about how much free space there is on the PC they are using. However, when SAS programs are run under z/OS on a mainframe machine, the correct use of disk space for WORK and permanent SAS data libraries is more complex, but essential to their smooth running. This chapter describes various methods of exploiting the space available on a mainframe, but also considers how some of these methods can be applied to other platforms like Windows, Linux, and UNIX.

2.2 Introduction

To demonstrate the similarities and differences between PC SAS and z/OS mainframe SAS systems, I have included a quick comparison of PC and z/OS mainframe terms here:

PC	z/OS Mainframe
RAM, e.g., 512Mb (1 user)	Region, e.g., 256Mb (100s of users)
Hard drive, e.g., 40Gb (10s, or less)	DASD, or disk volume, e.g., 2.5Gb (100s, or more)
DAT, e.g., 4Gb (10s)	Tape, e.g., 2Gb (1000s)

Unlike other platforms for SAS software, when you create a file under z/OS, you must specify the initial and maximum amounts of disk space you require, in advance. If this is not done correctly, either the file will run out of space prematurely if you specify too small an amount, or the file will not be created at all if you specify an initial size that is bigger than the free space on any of the available disk volumes.

The space-saving techniques described here are not all exclusively for the mainframe. Techniques that are applicable to other platforms, including Windows and UNIX, will be indicated.

2.3 Space Allocation under z/OS

Space allocation under z/OS is made up of two distinct parts:

- Primary allocation determines how big the file will be when it is first created, and hence, determines which disk volume it will be created on (i.e., one that has free space big enough to receive the new file). It should be noted that the initial space allocation can be satisfied using up to four separate pieces called extents. If more than four extents are required to complete the primary allocation, then the creation fails.

- Secondary allocations, or extents, are used when the file has additional data written to it so that the original allocation is not big enough to hold all the data. Up to a total of 16 extents, including the primary allocation, can be created for a file containing a SAS data library, but the size of each additional extent may be reduced if the biggest contiguous section of free space on the disk volume is smaller than the secondary allocation size.

There are four basic units of space used when allocating a SAS data library under z/OS, i.e., CYL (1 cylinder = approx. 0.75Mb), TRK (15 tracks = 1 cylinder), BLK (blocks = file blocksize), and bytes. In general, SAS data libraries tend to be allocated in cylinders or blocks, e.g.:

```
OPTIONS BLKSIZE(DISK)=OPT;
LIBNAME libref 'project.group.type' DISP=(NEW,CATLG)
  SPACE=(CYL,(10,5));
DATA libref.newfile;
  SET lib.master;
  .....data processing.....
RUN;
```

The preceding example shows the creation of a SAS data library called 'project.group.type' with a primary allocation of 10 cylinders, and additional secondary allocations of 5 cylinders each. Because no record format information was specified, SAS software will create the data library in an optimal allocation, using a record format of FS (Fixed Spanned), with logical record length and blocksize suitable for the type of disk volume used, i.e., for 3,390 devices, these would both be 27,648 bytes. In general, increasing the blocksize will reduce the disk space required to store the data, because there will be fewer blocks of data per megabyte of disk and hence fewer inter-block gaps, which are used to separate and identify the individual blocks of data.

2.3.1 Reallocation of Space under z/OS

Some implementations of system storage managers, such as HSM (hierarchical storage manager), can affect the primary allocations of SAS data libraries. In particular, when a SAS data library is archived and restored, it is returned to a disk volume in a single primary extent, which, if it previously had secondary extents before the archiving, will be larger than originally specified. The secondary allocation size will not be affected.

2.3.2 Common z/OS Disk Space Errors

Most z/OS error codes related to having insufficient disk space to expand the SAS data library end in 37, e.g., SB37, SD37, and SE37. This is caused by not allocating enough space for the amount of data being written to it. However, the amount of data actually being written may be greater than anticipated for several reasons:

- The code is looping around an OUTPUT statement.

- A PROC SQL join is generating every possible combination of each row in one SAS data set with rows in another SAS data set.

- A piece of SAS code used to select specific rows is not being executed, or is selecting every row.

2.4 Saving Permanent Disk Space

Permanent disk space is used for storing SAS data to be retained after the SAS session has ended.

2.4.1 Creating a SAS Data Set (All Platforms)

There are many ways a SAS data set can be created but, by default, the resulting data set will contain every column input to, and created by, the DATA step processing. It is probable that some of these columns will not be used again in the program, so the space occupied by these columns is just being wasted. To save space, keep the columns you require in a DATA step, select the columns you require in PROC SQL, or drop the columns you do not need later in a DATA step, e.g.:

```
DATA lib.newfile (KEEP=needed1 needed3 needed5);
  SET lib.master;
   .....data processing.....
RUN;
```
or

```
DATA lib.newfile;
  SET lib.master;
  KEEP needed1 needed3 needed5;
   .....data processing.....
RUN;
```
or

```
PROC SQL;
  CREATE TABLE lib.newfile AS
    SELECT needed1, needed3, needed5 FROM lib.master;
QUIT;
```
or
```
DATA lib.newfile (DROP=temp2 temp4 temp9);
  SET lib.master;
  .....data processing.....
RUN;
```
or
```
DATA lib.newfile;
  SET lib.master;
  DROP temp2 temp4 temp9;
  .....data processing.....
RUN;
```

2.4.2 Replacing a SAS Data Set (All Platforms)

If the output SAS data set from a processing step already exists, then to preserve the old data set from premature destruction, the new data set is created in free space within the SAS data library. Only when the processing step has successfully finished creating the new data set, is the old data set deleted, and the space it occupied is added to the free space. This means that whenever a data set is copied within a SAS data library, there must be sufficient free space available to store another copy of that data set, and the original data gets moved to a completely different area within the data library as a result of this processing.

2.4.3 Appending to a SAS Data Set (All Platforms)

If you do not want to rewrite the SAS data set every time it needs new rows added to it, try appending the new rows to the end of the data set using PROC APPEND, e.g.:

```
DATA newrecs;
  column1='ABC123';
  column2=42;
  OUTPUT;
  column1='ABD153';
  column2=47;
  OUTPUT;
RUN;
PROC APPEND BASE=lib.master DATA=newrecs;
RUN;
```

Note that PROC APPEND expects the BASE= and DATA= SAS data sets to have exactly the same columns. The FORCE= option should be used to enable a data set that contains new rows with differing columns to be appended to the master data set without generating errors.

2.4.4 Inserting and Deleting Observations (All Platforms)

PROC SQL can be used to insert or delete rows within a SAS data set. The INSERT SQL statement works in a similar way to PROC APPEND, by adding new rows at the end of the current data set. Any columns not specified in the INSERT statement are filled with missing values when the new row is written to the SAS data set. The DELETE SQL statement will mark individual rows as deleted, but it does not remove the data from the SAS data set. This means that, over time, the number of undeleted rows may not change dramatically, but the size of the SAS data set will continue to increase. The only way to clean out the rows marked as deleted is to copy the data set to a new location, e.g.:

```
DATA work.master;
  SET lib.master;
RUN;
DATA lib.master;
  SET work.master;
RUN;
```

or

```
PROC SQL;
  CREATE TABLE work.master AS SELECT * FROM lib.master;
  CREATE TABLE lib.master AS SELECT * FROM work.master;
QUIT;
```

or

```
PROC COPY IN=lib OUT=work;
  SELECT master;
RUN;
PROC COPY IN=work OUT=lib;
  SELECT master;
RUN;
```

2.5 Saving Temporary Disk Space

Temporary disk space is used to store intermediate SAS data. However, at the end of the SAS session, this disk space is returned to the pool of temporary disk space and the data is lost.

2.5.1 Creating Multiple SAS Data Sets in the Same DATA Step (All Platforms)

The following code has been included here to help to explain the code used later in this chapter. The technique of creating multiple SAS data sets in a single DATA step is not really a space-saving technique, but it will reduce the amount of data read, because for each row read, there can be many rows written in several different data sets. The only other method available would be to read the input data set individually for each output data set created, e.g.:

```
DATA lib.file1 lib.file2 lib.file3;
   SET lib.master;
   .....data processing.....
   IF type=1 THEN OUTPUT lib.file1;
   ELSE IF type=2 THEN OUTPUT lib.file2;
   ELSE OUTPUT lib.file3;
RUN;
```

2.5.2 WORK Allocation

There is a standard notation for z/OS temporary files, e.g., &temp, which should not be confused with SAS macro variables but instead should be written inside single quotation marks to prevent them from being resolved by SAS.

By default, SAS software allocates a WORK data library with the library reference of WORK. However, it is possible to allocate many library references to temporary work volumes, thereby allowing the operating system to spread the WORK data sets across many volumes, e.g. (using the z/OS temporary file notation):

```
LIBNAME work01 '&temp1' UNIT=sysda SPACE=(CYL,(100,100));
LIBNAME work02 '&temp2' UNIT=sysda SPACE=(CYL,(100,100));
LIBNAME work03 '&temp3' UNIT=sysda SPACE=(CYL,(100,100));
```

You can then write your temporary SAS data sets to one or other of the WORK data libraries, e.g.:

```
DATA work01.file1 work02.file2 work03.file3;
  SET lib.master;
  IF type=1 THEN OUTPUT work01.file1;
  ELSE IF type=2 THEN OUTPUT work02.file2;
  ELSE OUTPUT work03.file3;
RUN;
```

2.5.3 SORTWORK Allocation

By default, in batch jobs SAS software allocates three SORTWORK files: SORTWK01, SORTWK02, and SORTWK03, which provide an overflow working space for PROC SORT and other SAS procedures that order the data. In interactive SAS, there are no SORTWORK files allocated by default. The SAS system option SORTWKNO can be used to change this number to a maximum of 6, and spread the SORTWORK overflow, e.g.:

```
OPTIONS SORTWKNO=6;
```

The SAS system option SORT is used to change the minimum total size of SORTWORK data sets and defaults to 0 interactively and 4 in batch. It is measured in the units specified by the SAS system option SORTUNIT, which defaults to CYLS, e.g.:

```
OPTIONS SORT=10;
```

However, if you find you need to change these SAS system options in interactive SAS software, then it probably means that you ought to be executing this SAS program in batch anyway.

2.5.4 WORK and SORTWORK Allocation in Batch

The z/OS batch procedure for running SAS programs includes default allocations for WORK and SORTWORK in the JCL of the procedure. These defaults can be overridden with the following:

- JCL parameters, e.g.:

```
//STEP1 EXEC SAS, SORT=10
```

or

```
//STEP2 EXEC SAS, WORK='200,200'
```

- Additional overriding JCL DD cards, e.g.:

```
//STEP3 EXEC SAS
//WORK DD UNIT=SYSDA,SPACE=(CYL,(100,100))
```

- Both JCL parameters and additional JCL DD cards, e.g.:

```
//STEP4 EXEC SAS, OPTIONS='SORTWKNO=4'
//SORTWK04 DD UNIT=SYSDA,SPACE=(CYL,(10,10))
```

2.5.5 Virtual Disk Space

z/OS provides an alternative to physical disk space by emulating the disk space in virtual memory, e.g. (using the z/OS temporary file notation):

```
LIBNAME vdisk '&tempvio' UNIT=VIO SPACE=(CYL,(100,100))
```

In isolation, these virtual disks (VIO) are much quicker than physical disks, but care should be exercised in using them on a system that supports large numbers of interactive users, because virtual memory is large but finite. Some system administrators may restrict the use of virtual disks during periods of high interactive use, but encourage their use overnight, or in batch windows, when memory is more readily available.

2.5.6 Reusing WORK Data Set Names and Other Housekeeping (All Platforms)

How many times have you run a SAS program that uses WORK data sets for storing intermediate data and then run out of space in your WORK data library before the end?

The data stored in these WORK data sets is probably needed for only a small section of the program, and then it sits there unused for the remainder of the run, wasting vast amounts of WORK space. If you were to reuse some of the names of these WORK data sets later in the SAS program, then you would effectively recycle their disk space, enabling you to temporarily save more data, e.g.:

```
DATA file10;
  SET file9;
  .....data processing.....
RUN;
DATA file9;
  SET file10;
  .....more data processing.....
RUN;
```

Alternatively, you could delete all your WORK data sets after you have finished with them, either individually, e.g.:

```
PROC DATASETS LIB=work;
  DELETE file9 file10;
RUN;
```

or all at once, e.g.:

```
PROC DATASETS LIB=work KILL;
RUN;
```

2.6 General Disk Space Economies

The following information has been included to supplement the suggestions for saving permanent and temporary disk space. In some cases, you should not use this information to save disk space unless there would be additional benefits associated with any changes made.

2.6.1 Tape Format SAS Data Sets

The typical SAS data library on disk is allocated so that the data can be accessed at random, and includes a directory inside to point to the positions of individual SAS data sets and other SAS objects within the data library. This additional information increases the size of the data library and prevents it from becoming larger than the size of a single disk volume.

If a SAS data library is created on a tape, the TAPE engine is automatically used to create a special sequential-format SAS data library. This format can only be written or read sequentially, which restricts the user to accessing a single SAS data set from any individual sequential-format SAS data library. However, a sequential-format SAS data library can be written across more than one tape volume.

It is possible to create sequential-format SAS data libraries on disk volumes, instead of tape volumes, by using the TAPE engine keyword in the LIBNAME statement when creating a new SAS data library, e.g.:

```
LIBNAME libref TAPE 'project.group.type' SPACE=(CYL,(10,10))
  DISP=(NEW,CATLG);
```

However, sequential-format SAS data libraries that are allocated on disk volumes occupy about 50% more disk space than their equivalent standard SAS data libraries, so they are recommended for tape storage only.

2.6.2 Transport Format SAS Data Sets (All Platforms)

Standard SAS data sets on different platforms are structured in such a way that a binary copy from one platform to another is likely to create an unreadable file on the target platform. To alleviate this problem, SAS provides two different file formats that can be used to transfer SAS data sets from platform to platform.

2.6.3 XPORT Engine Files (All Platforms)

These files can be created using a LIBNAME statement with the XPORT engine a parameter. It is recommended that a record format of FB, a record length of 80, and a block size of 8,000 be used for the file. This format enables SAS to read and write data in the file by only the library reference. While this format is very straightforward to use, the transportability results in an increase in size of up to 15%.

When using the XPORT data libraries it should be noted that, although it is possible to store more than one data set in each library, because they can only be accessed sequentially, two data sets from the same XPORT library cannot be read in the same DATA step. There is also a compatibility issue with SAS 8 data set names, because XPORT data sets are still limited to eight characters, like SAS 6.12 data sets.

```
LIBNAME trans XPORT 'project.group.type' SPACE=(CYL,(10,10))
   DISP=(NEW,CATLG) LRECL=80 RECFM=FB BLKSIZE=8000;
PROC COPY IN=lib.master OUT=trans;
RUN;
```

Under Windows, the same example would look like the following:

```
LIBNAME trans XPORT 'c:\project\xport.xpt' LRECL=80 RECFM=F
   BLKSIZE=8000;
PROC COPY IN=lib.master OUT=trans;
RUN;
```

Under Linux or UNIX, the same example would look like the following:

```
LIBNAME trans XPORT '~/project/xport.xpt' LRECL=80 RECFM=F
   BLKSIZE=8000;
PROC COPY IN=lib.master OUT=trans;
RUN;
```

2.6.4 PROC CPORT and PROC CIMPORT Files (All Platforms)

These files can only be created using the SAS CPORT procedure writing to target files allocated using a FILENAME statement. Like the XPORT engine files, it is recommended that a record format of FB, a record length of 80, and a block size of 8,000 be used for the file. This format can only be read by SAS software once it has been converted back to a standard SAS format using the SAS CIMPORT procedure. The files can be smaller than the original SAS data libraries by as much as 40%, provided they do not contain a high proportion of nonzero and non-missing numeric values.

```
FILENAME cport 'project.group.type' SPACE=(CYL,(10,10))
  DISP=(NEW,CATLG) LRECL=80 RECFM=FB BLKSIZE=8000;
PROC CPORT DATA=lib.master FILE=cport;
RUN;
```

Under Windows, the same example would look like the following:

```
FILENAME cport 'c:\project\cport.trn' LRECL=80 RECFM=F
  BLKSIZE=8000;
PROC CPORT DATA=lib.master FILE=cport;
RUN;
```

Under Linux or UNIX, the same example would look like the following:

```
FILENAME cport '~/project/cport.trn' LRECL=80 RECFM=F
  BLKSIZE=8000;
PROC CPORT DATA=lib.master FILE=cport;
RUN;
```

2.6.5 Releasing Unused Space in a SAS Data Library

Finally, if you want to save some space on a disk volume in advance of the archiving system's nightly cleanup, then PROC RELEASE will enable you to release the unused space at the end of the SAS data library to an extent boundary, e.g.:

```
LIBNAME libref CLEAR;
FILENAME fileref 'project.group.type' DISP=OLD;
PROC RELEASE DDNAME=fileref EXTENTS;
RUN;
```

Note that it will not release free space from the middle of the data library. The simplest method of freeing all the unused disk space from within a SAS data library is to create a new SAS data library, copy all the SAS objects from the old data library to the new with PROC COPY, delete the old data library, rename the new data library to the name of the old one, and finally run PROC RELEASE to release any unused space at the end of the new data library. The SAS objects will be located at the beginning of the new SAS data library as they are copied over.

This saving can also be achieved when allocating a SAS data library using the RLSE option in the SPACE parameter, e.g.:

```
LIBNAME libref 'project.group.type' DISP=(NEW,CATLG)
    SPACE=(CYL,(10,10),RLSE);
```

2.6.6 Compression (All Platforms)

In SAS 6.12 you could choose among COMPRESS=NO (the default setting), COMPRESS=YES, SAS System, and data set option. COMPRESS=YES, resulting in compression ratios of up to 50%, could be achieved on SAS data sets that contain mostly numeric data and a high proportion of zero and missing values, which could increase to 80% or more for SAS data sets that contain mostly character fields having a large proportion of blanks. However, a high proportion of nonzero and non-missing numeric values could result in the compression process increasing the size of the SAS data set.

In SAS 8 the choices were increased to COMPRESS=NO (the default setting), COMPRESS=BINARY, and COMPRESS=CHAR (also written as COMPRESS=YES). There was also a safety net introduced at the same time to prevent the compression process, actually significantly increasing the size of the SAS data set. In this case the potential increase in size is recorded in the SAS log with a warning message that compression has not been enabled, and the SAS data set is physically stored as an uncompressed file.

Like all benefits, there can be a price to pay, because the savings in disk space can cause an increase in the user CPU time required to read the data because the compressed data has to be decompressed before it can be read. However, there may still be a decrease in the overall CPU time measured (user CPU + system CPU) if the I/O processing (system CPU) time is dramatically reduced as a result of the reduced file size. The following table lists the results from disk space and CPU measurements made on a SAS 8.2 session running under Windows 2000 Service Pack 2 using NTFS disk formatting. Additional disk space savings due to NTFS disk compression, which was the default setting for the files and folders used, are also listed.

Disk Space-Saving Method	Measurement	Numeric Zero	Numeric Missing	Numeric Random	Text Blank	Text Random
COMPRESS = NO	Actual kilobytes	2369	2369	2369	26673	26673
	NTFS kilobytes	152	152	2369	1672	5004
	User CPU time	0.1	0.1	0.07	1.09	0.96
	System CPU time	0.42	0.31	0.39	4.43	3.91
COMPRESS = BINARY	Actual kilobytes	193	841	2521[1]	193	2881
	NTFS kilobytes	52	160	2512	48	1216
	User CPU time	0.09	0.4	0.1	0.64	1.47
	System CPU time	0.27	0.18	0.32	2.19	2.54
COMPRESS = CHAR	Actual kilobytes	157	1621	2521[1]	209	11297
	NTFS kilobytes	40	108	2512	48	2412
	User CPU time	0.12	0.3	0.14	0.57	1.06
	System CPU time	0.36	0.22	0.24	2.43	3.61
XPORT Engine	Actual kilobytes	2349	2349	2349	23442	23442
	NTFS kilobytes	4	148	2349	1468	4396
	User CPU time	0.52	0.42	0.47	2.09	1.81
	System CPU time	0.28	0.23	0.42	2.99	3.18
PROC CPORT	Actual kilobytes	412	1233	2706	969	10805
	NTFS kilobytes	52	156	2706	124	2112
	User CPU time	0.17+0.16	0.17+0.07	0.24+0.1	0.44+0.95	0.76+0.98
	System CPU time	0.04+0.2	0.08+0.26	0.04+0.22	0.49+3.01	0.45+3.25

[1]**Note:** Compression increased disk space usage by 6.6%, and was not disabled because the compressed file was not determined to be obviously larger.

Examples of the SAS code used to measure the CPU time used to process the SAS data is given below. The timings recorded in the preceding table relate only to reading the data with %test_process and PROC CIMPORT, and not to the time used to create the data files. Note also that the PROC CIMPORT step is used only to read the data stored by the PROC CPORT processing.

```
LIBNAME lib ".\";
FILENAME cp_zero '.\zero_cport.cpt' LRECL=80 RECFM=f
  BLKSIZE=8000;
LIBNAME xp1zero XPORT '.\zero_xport.xpt';
LIBNAME xp2zero XPORT '.\zero_xport2.xpt';
LIBNAME xp3zero XPORT '.\zero_xport3.xpt';
LIBNAME xp4zero XPORT '.\zero_xport4.xpt';
LIBNAME xp5zero XPORT '.\zero_xport5.xpt';
DATA lib.zero_num (KEEP=zero1-zero30)
     lib.miss_num (KEEP=miss1-miss30)
     lib.rand_num (KEEP=rand1-rand30)
     lib.blank_ch (KEEP=blank1-blank30)
     lib.text_ch (KEEP=text1-text30)
     lib.zero_num_bin (KEEP=zero1-zero30 COMPRESS=BINARY)
     lib.miss_num_bin (KEEP=miss1-miss30 COMPRESS=BINARY)
     lib.rand_num_bin (KEEP=rand1-rand30 COMPRESS=BINARY)
     lib.blank_ch_bin (KEEP=blank1-blank30 COMPRESS=BINARY)
     lib.text_ch_bin (KEEP=text1-text30 COMPRESS=BINARY)
     lib.zero_num_char (KEEP=zero1-zero30 COMPRESS=CHAR)
     lib.miss_num_char (KEEP=miss1-miss30 COMPRESS=CHAR)
     lib.rand_num_char (KEEP=rand1-rand30 COMPRESS=CHAR)
     lib.blank_ch_char (KEEP=blank1-blank30 COMPRESS=CHAR)
     lib.text_ch_char (KEEP=text1-text30 COMPRESS=CHAR)
     ;
  ARRAY zero_ [*] zero1-zero30;
  ARRAY miss_ [*] miss1-miss30;
  ARRAY rand_ [*] rand1-rand30;
  ARRAY blank_ [*] $80 blank1-blank30;
  ARRAY text_ [*] $80 text1-text30;
  DO i=1 TO 10000;
    DO j=1 TO dim(zero_);
      zero_[j]=0;
      miss_[j]=.;
      rand_[j]=RANUNI(0);
      blank_[j]=" ";
      text_[j]=PUT(i+j, WORDS80.);
    END;
    OUTPUT lib.zero_num lib.miss_num lib.rand_num
           lib.blank_ch lib.text_ch
           lib.zero_num_bin lib.miss_num_bin lib.rand_num_bin
           lib.blank_ch_bin lib.text_ch_bin
```

```
          lib.zero_num_char lib.miss_num_char
lib.rand_num_char
          lib.blank_ch_char lib.text_ch_char
          ;
  END;
  STOP;
RUN;
PROC CPORT DATA=lib.zero_num FILE=cp_zero;
RUN;
PROC COPY IN=lib OUT=xp1zero;
  SELECT zero_num;
RUN;
PROC COPY IN=lib OUT=xp2zero;
  SELECT zero_num;
RUN;
PROC COPY IN=lib OUT=xp3zero;
  SELECT zero_num;
RUN;
PROC COPY IN=lib OUT=xp4zero;
  SELECT zero_num;
RUN;
PROC COPY IN=lib OUT=xp5zero;
  SELECT zero_num;
RUN;
OPTIONS FULLSTIMER;
%MACRO test_process(dsn1,dsn2,dsn3,dsn4,dsn5);
  DATA x;
    SET &dsn1 &dsn2 &dsn3 &dsn4 &dsn5;
    value=1;
  RUN;
%MEND;
%test_process(lib.zero_num, lib.zero_num, lib.zero_num,
  lib.zero_num, lib.zero_num)
%test_process(lib.zero_num_bin, lib.zero_num_bin,
lib.zero_num_bin,
  lib.zero_num_bin, lib.zero_num_bin)
%test_process(lib.zero_num_char, lib.zero_num_char,
  lib.zero_num_char, lib.zero_num_char, lib.zero_num_char)
%test_process(xp1zero.zero_num, xp2zero.zero_num,
xp3zero.zero_num,
  xp4zero.zero_num, xp5zero.zero_num)
PROC CIMPORT DATA=zero_num FILE=cp_zero;
RUN;
%test_process(zero_num, zero_num, zero_num, zero_num, zero_num)
```

2.7 Recommendations

2.7.1 All Platforms

- Don't keep columns of data in SAS data sets that you will not use again. To cut down on unnecessary waste, use the KEEP= or DROP= options or the KEEP or DROP statements.

- Don't keep WORK data sets that you will not use again. Reuse their names, or better still, delete them altogether when you have finished using them, so that you can reuse the space they occupied.

- If you are running out of disk space, compress SAS data sets that contain high proportions of blank, zero, or missing values to make significant savings. However, be aware that there could be corresponding increases in CPU time to process these data sets, even if no disk space savings are seen.

2.7.2 z/OS Mainframe Specific

Plan your disk space usage in advance. z/OS files cannot be increased in size by user actions once they have been allocated. Only the automated system utilities can reallocate SAS data libraries, and do so by removing them from the disks and then re-creating them in a single extent.

2.8 Recommended Reading

For more information, go to www.hollandnumerics.com/books/Saving_Time_and_Money_using_SAS.htm. This page includes a chapter-by-chapter list of recommended reading.

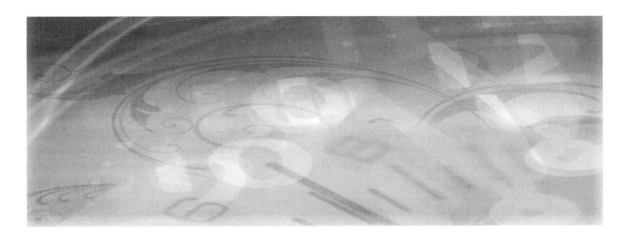

Chapter 3

Why Does My Job Run So Slowly?

3.1 Abstract

Almost every operation you are able to perform using SAS software can be achieved in many different ways, each with its own advantages and disadvantages. It is not always possible to predict the disadvantages, as a basic operation may be suitable in one circumstance but may be totally inappropriate in another. Using SAS/ACCESS software and PROC SQL gives you a wide variety of alternative methods, but in general, only one is likely to give a solution and a fast response time. This chapter explores these choices and gives insight into how to determine the most efficient approach.

3.2 Introduction to SAS/ACCESS Software

The SAS/ACCESS component of SAS software offers interfaces to access data in relational databases (e.g., DB2, Oracle, and Informix). In this chapter I will be concentrating on access to DB2 tables, but most of the examples could be applied in a similar way to other relational database systems.

I would like to consider, in particular, the choice to be made between access descriptors, Pass-Through SQL, and DB2 LIBNAME statements, and how much processing should be done in DB2 when designing the interface between SAS and DB2.

3.2.1 Access Descriptors versus Pass-Through SQL versus DB2 LIBNAME Statements

Access Descriptors

Here is an example of an access descriptor:

```
PROC ACCESS DBMS=db2;
  CREATE work.a.access;
  SSID=db2ssid;
  TABLE=db2a.db2table;
  ASSIGN=yes;
  CREATE work.b.view;
  SELECT ALL;
RUN;
```

Here are the advantages of access descriptors:

- Can be used to update, insert, and delete data in DB2 tables.
- Provide a simple interface to SAS, which makes the DB2 table look like a standard SAS data set.
- Can be used to perform DB2 queries that have been predefined.

Here are the disadvantages of access descriptors:

- When using an access descriptor, a copy of all the DB2 data described in the access descriptor is transferred to SAS before any processing can be performed by the SAS software.
- DB2 does not perform any optimization of the query defined by the access descriptor; i.e., there is no use made of any DB2 indexes.
- Cannot be used to perform DB2 queries that have not been predefined.
- Column names are limited to eight characters.

Pass-Through SQL

Here is an example of Pass-Through SQL:

```
PROC SQL;
  CONNECT to db2 (SSID=db2ssid);
  CREATE VIEW work.c AS
    SELECT *
    FROM   CONNECTION to db2
           (SELECT *
             FROM   db2a.db2table);
  DISCONNECT from db2;
QUIT;
```

Here are the advantages of Pass-Through SQL:

- Can be used to perform DB2 queries that have not been predefined.
- DB2 can optimize the query to use DB2 indexes.
- Can be used to execute any DB2 SQL statements, including the updating, inserting, and deleting of data in DB2 tables, and the creating, modifying, and deleting of DB2 tables, provided the user has permission to perform these actions.
- Supports long column names.

Here are the disadvantages of Pass-Through SQL:

- DB2 SQL syntax must be understood.

DB2 LIBNAME Statements

There is an example of a DB2 LIBNAME statement:

```
LIBNAME db2lib DB2 SSID=db2ssid;
```

Here are the advantages of DB2 LIBNAME statements:

- Can be used to update, insert, and delete data in DB2 tables.
- Provide a simple interface to SAS, which makes the DB2 table look like a standard SAS data set.
- Can be used to perform DB2 queries that have been predefined.
- Supports long column names.

Here are the disadvantages of DB2 LIBNAME statements:

- Cannot be used to perform DB2 queries that have not been predefined.

3.3 PROC SQL

This book is not intended as a tutorial on PROC SQL, but the following SQL constructions need to be explained here to clarify the discussion later in this chapter. The SQL syntax used in this chapter is compatible with both PROC SQL within SAS and in DB2 Version 4 and later.

Figure 3.1 PROC SQL Joins

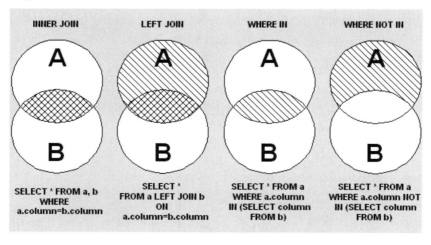

3.3.1 Processing Data in DB2 or in SAS?

Summarizing Rows in a DB2 Table

Figure 3.2 Counting Rows in a DB2 Table

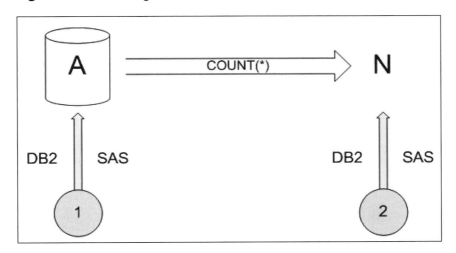

Here is sample code for Figure 3.2:

(1a) Pass-Through SQL:

```
PROC SQL;
  CONNECT TO db2 (SSID=db2ssid);
  SELECT COUNT(*) FROM CONNECTION TO db2 (SELECT * FROM a);
  DISCONNECT FROM db2;
QUIT;
```

(1b) Access Descriptor:

```
PROC ACCESS DBMS=db2;
  CREATE work.asas1.access;
  SSID=db2ssid;
  TABLE=userid.a;
  ASSIGN=yes;
  CREATE work.asas.view;
  SELECT ALL;
RUN;
```

```
PROC SQL NOPRINT;
  SELECT COUNT(*)
  FROM   work.asas;
QUIT;
```

(1c) DB2 LIBNAME Statement:

```
LIBNAME db2sas1 DB2 SSID=db2ssid;

PROC SQL NOPRINT;
  SELECT COUNT(*)
  FROM   db2sas1.a;
QUIT;
```

(2) Pass-Through SQL:

```
PROC SQL;
  CONNECT TO db2 (SSID=db2ssid);
  SELECT * FROM CONNECTION TO db2 (SELECT COUNT(*)FROM a);
  DISCONNECT FROM db2;
QUIT;
```

The results in CPU seconds are given here:

Rows (a)	SAS Version	1a	1b	1c	2
517,000	9.1.3 on z/OS	15.27	7.92	0.18	0.18

Combining Subsets of Two DB2 Tables

This example uses data from two DB2 tables of different sizes, one larger than the other. The tables will be joined using a column on each table that is indexed in DB2, and then the joined table is subset with a WHERE clause. The designing of a query on several DB2 tables from SAS needs to include consideration of when the data will be transferred to the SAS environment for manipulation by the SAS software.

Figure 3.3 Subsetting and Merging DB2 Tables

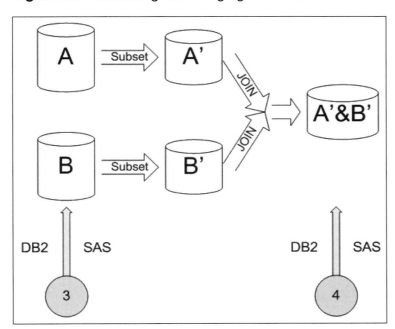

Here is sample code for Figure 3.3:

(3a) Access Descriptor:

```
PROC ACCESS DBMS=db2;
  CREATE work.bsas1.access;
  SSID=db2ssid;
  TABLE=userid.b;
  ASSIGN=yes;
  CREATE work.bsas.view;
  SELECT ALL;
RUN;

PROC ACCESS DBMS=db2;
  CREATE work.asas1.access;
  SSID=db2ssid;
  TABLE=userid.a;
  ASSIGN=yes;
  CREATE work.asas.view;
  SELECT ALL;
RUN;
```

```
PROC SQL NOPRINT;
  SELECT *
  FROM    work.bsas
          ,work.asas
  WHERE   bsas.account=asas.account
    AND   bsas.time=asas.time
    AND   asas.trans IN ('0123','4567','8901')
    AND   asas.code_cf = 'C'
  ORDER BY
          bsas.account
          ,bsas.number;
QUIT;
```

(3b) DB2 LIBNAME Statement:

```
LIBNAME db2sas2 DB2 SSID=db2ssid;

PROC SQL NOPRINT;
  SELECT b.*
  FROM    db2sas2.b
          ,db2sas2.a
  WHERE   b.account=a.account
    AND   b.time=a.time
    AND   a.trans IN ('0123','4567','8901')
    AND   a.code_cf = 'C'
  ORDER BY
          b.account
          ,b.number;
QUIT;
```

(4) Pass-Through SQL:

```
PROC SQL NOPRINT;
  CONNECT TO db2 (SSID=db2ssid);
  SELECT *
  FROM    CONNECTION TO db2
          (SELECT b.*
                  ,a.time AS atime
            FROM    b
                    ,a
            WHERE   b.account=a.account
              AND   b.time=a.time
              AND   a.trans IN ('0123','4567','8901')
              AND   a.code_cf = 'C') AS d
```

```
ORDER BY
        d.account
        ,d.number;
DISCONNECT FROM db2;
QUIT;
```

Figure 3.4 Merging and Subsetting DB2 Tables

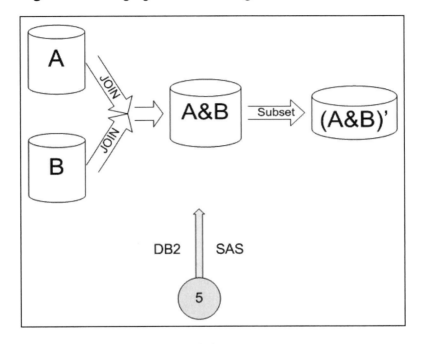

Here is sample code for Figure 3.4:

(5) Pass-Through SQL:

```
PROC SQL NOPRINT;
  CONNECT TO db2 (SSID=db2ssid);
  SELECT *
  FROM    CONNECTION TO db2
          (SELECT b.*
                  ,a.time AS atime
            FROM    b
                   ,a
           WHERE   b.account=a.account
             AND   b.time=a.time) AS d
  WHERE   d.trans IN ('0123','4567','8901')
    AND   d.code_cf = 'C'
```

```
ORDER BY
        d.account
        ,d.number;
    DISCONNECT FROM db2;
QUIT;
```

The results in CPU seconds are given here:

Rows (a)	Rows (b)	SAS Version	3a	3b	4	5
517,000	20,000	9.1.3 on z/OS	8.74	2.83	9.21	25.21
517,000	20,000	6.09e on MVS	535.90	n/a	0.80	15.70
517,000	98,000	6.09e on MVS	541.11	n/a	46.60	856.30
120,000	20,000	6.09e on MVS	74.00	n/a	25.00	30.60
120,000	98,000	6.09e on MVS	184.80	n/a	87.80	115.00

Adding Extra Information to a DB2 Table from Another DB2 Table

This example uses data from two DB2 tables indexed using the same columns. To add additional information to the first table, where there may or may not be a matching record in the second table, it is best to use the left join, preferably making use of indexed columns for matching the two tables.

Figure 3.5 Subsetting and Left Joining DB2 Tables

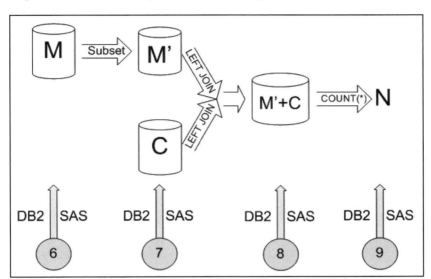

Here is sample code for Figure 3.5:

(6a) Access Descriptor:

```
PROC ACCESS DBMS=db2;
  CREATE work.msas1.access;
  SSID=db2ssid;
  TABLE=userid.m;
  ASSIGN=yes;
  CREATE work.msas.view;
  SELECT ALL;
RUN;

PROC ACCESS DBMS=db2;
  CREATE work.csas1.access;
  SSID=db2ssid;
  TABLE=userid.c;
  ASSIGN=yes;
  CREATE work.csas.view;
  SELECT ALL;
RUN;
```

```
PROC SQL NOPRINT;
  SELECT COUNT(*)
  FROM    (SELECT *
           FROM    work.msas
           WHERE   SUBSTR(code,1,1) = 'A') as msas1
  LEFT JOIN
          work.csas
  ON      msas1.account=csas.account
    AND   msas1.time=csas.time;
QUIT;
```

(6b) DB2 LIBNAME Statement:

```
LIBNAME db2sas3 DB2 SSID=db2ssid;

PROC SQL NOPRINT;
  SELECT COUNT(*)
  FROM    db2sas3.m msas1
  LEFT JOIN
          db2sas3.c
  ON      msas1.account=c.account
    AND   msas1.time=c.time
  WHERE   SUBSTR(code,1,1) = 'A';
QUIT;
```

(7) Pass-Through SQL:

```
PROC SQL NOPRINT;
  CONNECT TO db2 (SSID=db2ssid);
  CREATE VIEW work.msas AS
    SELECT *
    FROM    CONNECTION TO db2
            (SELECT *
             FROM    m
             WHERE   SUBSTR(code,1,1) = 'A');
  CREATE VIEW work.csas AS
    SELECT *
    FROM    CONNECTION TO db2
            (SELECT *
             FROM    c);
  SELECT COUNT(*)
  FROM    (SELECT *
           FROM    work.msas) AS msas
  LEFT JOIN
          work.csas
```

```
      ON      msas.account=csas.account
        AND  msas.time=csas.time;
      DISCONNECT FROM db2;
   QUIT;
```

(8) Pass-Through SQL:

```
   PROC SQL NOPRINT;
     CONNECT TO db2 (SSID=db2ssid);
     SELECT COUNT(*)
     FROM   CONNECTION TO db2
            (SELECT *
             FROM   (SELECT *
                     FROM    m
                     WHERE   SUBSTR(code,1,1) = 'A') AS m1
             LEFT JOIN
                    c
             ON     m1.account=c.account
               AND  m1.time=c.time);
     DISCONNECT FROM db2;
   QUIT;
```

(9) Pass-Through SQL:

```
   PROC SQL NOPRINT;
     CONNECT TO db2 (SSID=db2ssid.);
     SELECT *
     FROM   CONNECTION TO db2
            (SELECT COUNT(*)
             FROM   (SELECT *
                     FROM    m
                     WHERE   SUBSTR(code,1,1) = 'A') AS m1
             LEFT JOIN
                    c
             ON     m1.account=c.account
               AND  m1.time=c.time);
     DISCONNECT FROM db2;
   QUIT;
```

Figure 3.6 Left Joining and Subsetting DB2 Tables

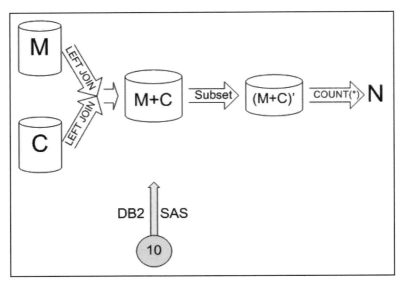

Here is sample code for Figure 3.6:

(10) Pass-Through SQL:

```
PROC SQL NOPRINT;
  CONNECT TO db2 (SSID=db2ssid.);
  SELECT COUNT(*)
  FROM   CONNECTION TO db2
         (SELECT *
          FROM   m
          LEFT JOIN
                 c
          ON     m.account=c.account
            AND  m.time=c.time)
  WHERE  SUBSTR(code,1,1) = 'A';
  DISCONNECT FROM db2;
QUIT;
```

The results in CPU seconds are given here:

Rows (m)	Rows (c)	SAS Version	6a	6b	7	8	9	10
5,200,000	640,000	9.1.3 on z/OS	114.68	151.33	109.92	721.11	82.40	6,554.66
5,200,000	640,000	6.09e on MVS	1,394.00	n/a	461.40	397.40	146.70	2,282.40

Selecting Rows from a SAS Data Set Using Another SAS Data Set

This example uses data from two SAS data sets with common columns, but there are duplicate column values in both tables. Note that this process can also be performed in DB2. The rows from the first SAS data set will be selected if there is, or is not, a match between common columns. No additional information in the second table is required.

There were two SAS data sets used to measure the following results: AX (80,000 rows) and XC (52,000 rows).

Selecting Matching Rows

Here is sample code for selecting matching rows using the WHERE IN method:

```
SELECT * FROM ax WHERE column IN (SELECT column FROM xc);
```

There were 4,300 records produced in 4.1 seconds.

Here is sample code for selecting matching rows using the INNER JOIN method:

```
SELECT * FROM ax, xc WHERE ax.column=xc.column;
```

There were 10,595,900 records produced in 122.4 seconds.

Here is sample code for selecting matching rows using the DISTINCT INNER JOIN method:

```
SELECT DISTINCT * FROM ax, xc WHERE ax.column=xc.column;
```

There were 4,300 records produced in 303.8 seconds.

Selecting Missing Rows

Here is sample code for selecting missing rows using the WHERE NOT IN method:

```
SELECT * FROM ax WHERE column NOT IN (SELECT column FROM xc);
```

There were 75,600 records produced in 4.5 seconds.

Here is sample code for selecting missing rows using the DISTINCT LEFT JOIN method:

```
SELECT * FROM ax LEFT JOIN xc ON ax.column=xc.column
   WHERE xc.column=" ";
```

There were 75,600 records produced in 175.4 seconds.

3.4 Summary of Results

3.4.1 Summarizing Rows in a DB2 Table

The time taken to summarize the data decreases when most of the processing is performed in DB2 before transferring the result to SAS.

The preferred options here are (**1c**) and (**2**).

3.4.2 Combining DB2 Tables Using Inner Join or Left Join

As you saw earlier in the inner join, the time taken decreases as more processing is performed in DB2, but also in both the inner join and left join, the early subset of the data reduces the amount of data being passed through the DB2 to SAS interface.

The differences in relative timings between SAS 6 and SAS 9 probably indicate the improvements made in the DB2 to SAS interface since SAS 6. The preferred options here are (**3b**) and (**4**) for inner joins, and (**9**) for left joins.

3.4.3 Selecting Rows from a SAS Data Set Using Another SAS Data Set

Selecting Matching Rows

The presence of duplicate records in both base data sets and lookup data sets creates additional overhead when using the INNER JOIN method, because each duplicate record in one data set matches each duplicate record in the other, and removing these additional matches with the DISTINCT keyword can more than double the processing time. The WHERE IN method only has to scan the lookup SAS data set each time there is a new base record until the first match is found.

Selecting Missing Rows

The presence of duplicate records in both base data sets and lookup data sets creates additional overhead when using the LEFT JOIN method. The WHERE NOT IN method has to scan the full lookup SAS data set each time there is a new base record, if no match is found.

3.4.4 The Effects of Sorting with z/OS DFSORT

The following examples (A to F) demonstrate how DFSORT, the z/OS sort routine, can have a dramatic effect on the elapsed time of SAS programs.

SQL Joins versus PROC SORT and DATA Step Merges

In the next two examples (A and B), all the input tables are from DB2, and are read into SAS 8.2 using the DB2 LIBNAME engine, e.g.:

```
LIBNAME db2lib DB2 CONNECTION=SHAREDREAD DEFER=YES SSID=db01;
```

This statement creates a libref called **db2lib**, which will connect to the DB2 subsystem **db01**. CONNECTION=SHAREDREAD limits this libref to read-only access to DB2 tables. DEFER=YES delays the connection to the DB2 subsystem until a DB2 table is referenced by SAS. This feature is almost the same in both examples. In these examples, DB2 table **db2lib.dbt1** had 11.2 million records, and DB2 table **db2lib.dbt2** had 4.4 million records. The difference in observed speed can be attributed to the relative efficiencies of SQL internal matching algorithms and the DFSORT sort routine used by PROC SORT.

In general, on z/OS platforms SQL joins are more efficient than PROC SORT and DATA step merges if the input data sets are small, when PROC SORT will use its own sort routines, and less efficient if data sets are large, when SAS can compensate for any overhead of using external routines by the improved performance of sorting with the highly optimized DFSORT routine.

Title	SAS Code	Elapsed Time
[A] Original SAS code	```PROC SQL; CREATE TABLE new AS SELECT dbt1.key1 ,dbt1.column1 ,dbt2.column2 FROM db2lib.dbt1 LEFT JOIN db2lib.dbt2 ON dbt1.key1 = dbt2.key1; QUIT;```	3 hours
[B] Convert SQL LEFT JOIN into two PROC SORT steps and a DATA step merge	```PROC SORT DATA = db2lib.dbt1 OUT = sas1; BY key1; RUN; PROC SORT DATA = db2lib.dbt2 OUT = sas2; BY key1; RUN; DATA new (KEEP = key1 column1 column2); MERGE sas1 (IN = i1) sas2 (IN = i2); BY key1; IF i1; RUN;```	30 minutes

Data Step Merges Using Unsorted, Sorted, and Indexed Data Sets

The next four examples (C to F) highlight the dangers of assuming that, because SAS code works well using small data set sizes, that code can be scaled up indefinitely. Here SAS data set **SAS3** had 4.3 million records, and indexed SAS data set **SAS4**. The clue to the inefficiency of example C is in the massive EXCP count. The dramatic improvement in example D suggests that data set SAS3 was not sorted, so each request for a match from the indexed data set SAS4 returned a block of adjacent records, which were rarely, if ever, reused by the next request. Just sorting data set SAS3 in example D increased the reuse of each block returned from data set SAS4 at least 500-fold.

Comparison of example D with example E demonstrates how DATA step merges are more efficient than key lookups for data sets of around the same size. Key lookups are usually recommended when the indexed data set is much smaller than the main input data set.

Finally, example F is slower than example E because sorting an indexed data set with PROC SORT is more expensive than any gains achieved by merging two sorted data sets, even though the EXCP count is reduced nearly fourfold. However, the time spent creating an index for a data set will be worthwhile only if that data set is reused several times during its lifetime.

Title	SAS Code	Elapsed Time	EXCP Count

[C] Original SAS code	```DATA new (KEEP = key1 column1 column2);```
	```SET sas3;```
	``` SET sas4 KEY = key1;```
	```RUN;```
		7 hours	10,131,444

[D] Presort data set **SAS3**, but continue to use the key lookup on the indexed data set **SAS4**	```PROC SORT DATA = sas3;```
	``` BY key1;```
	```RUN;```
	```DATA new (KEEP = key1 column1 column2);```
	```SET sas3;```
	``` SET sas4 KEY = key1;```
	```RUN;```
		3 minutes 33 seconds	21,259

[E] Presort data set **SAS3**, and merge with the indexed data set **SAS4** in a DATA step	```PROC SORT DATA = sas3;```
	``` BY key1;```
	```RUN;```
	```DATA new (KEEP = key1 column1 column2);```
	```MERGE sas3 (IN = i1)```
	``` sas4 (IN = i2);```
	``` BY key1;```
	``` IF i1;```
	```RUN;```
		2 minutes 50 seconds	21,332

[F] Presort data sets **SAS3** and **SAS4**, and merge the two sorted data sets in a DATA step	```PROC SORT DATA = sas3;```
	``` BY key1;```
	```RUN;```
	```PROC SORT DATA = sas4;```
	``` BY key1;```
	```RUN;```
	```DATA new (KEEP = key1 column1 column2);```
	```MERGE sas3 (IN = i1)```
	``` sas4 (IN = i2);```
	``` BY key1;```
	``` IF i1;```
	```RUN;```
		3 minutes 51 seconds	5,708

3.5 Converting SAS/ACCESS View Descriptors to SQL Views

It is recommended that you convert your SAS/ACCESS view descriptors to PROC SQL views, because this will enable you to use the LIBNAME statement, which can handle long column names. PROC SQL views are also platform-dependent, whereas SAS/ACCESS view descriptors are not. You can use the CV2VIEW procedure in SAS 9 to generate code that will create PROC SQL views, e.g.:

```
PROC CV2VIEW DBMS = db2;
   FROM_VIEW = inlib.accview (ALTER = apwd);
   TO_VIEW = outlib.sqlview;
   SAVEAS = 'sql.sas';
   REPLACE FILE;
RUN;
```

PROC CV2VIEW will convert both 64-bit SAS/ACCESS view descriptors created in SAS 9 or SAS 8, and 32-bit SAS/ACCESS descriptors created in SAS 8. However, it may not convert 32-bit SAS/ACCESS view descriptors created in SAS 6.12, in which case they must first be converted to compatible view descriptors in SAS 8.2.

3.6 Recommendations

- The LEFT JOIN method has been available since DB2 Version 4, which removes the need to perform separate WHERE NOT IN and INNER JOIN processes in DB2, then combining the fragments in SAS.

- If duplicate values exist in the column used for matching, then avoid joining the tables. If no additional information is needed from one of the tables, then use WHERE IN or WHERE NOT IN processing to just select the records required.

- Access descriptors are designed for simple updating of small DB2 tables using SAS/FSP or SAS/AF applications and utilities. Do not use access descriptors for reading large DB2 tables.

- If possible, sort the main data set to be combined with a second indexed data set by that index key, because this will maximize the number of matching records in a block returned by each lookup request, allowing reuse of the returned block of adjacent records.

- Use DATA step merges, rather than key lookups, when the key lookup data set is comparable in size to the main data set.

3.7 Recommended Reading

For more information, go to www.hollandnumerics.com/books/Saving_Time_and_Money_using_SAS.htm. This page includes a chapter-by-chapter list of recommended reading.

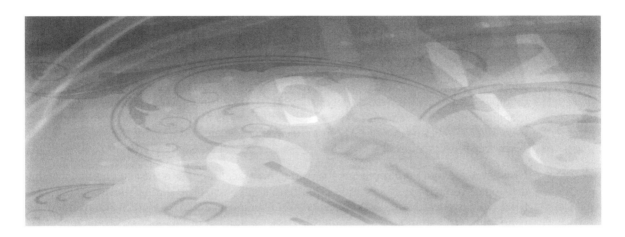

Chapter 4

Distributing SAS/GRAPH Reports

4.1 Abstract

The early releases of SAS/GRAPH software were used on large mainframe computers, and its device drivers catered almost exclusively to the dot-matrix and pen plotters, or to dumb terminals, which were widely used at the time for graphical reporting. If a graphical report was required to be distributed around a business, it would be stored in a SAS/GRAPH catalog, and a SAS program would be executed to reprint the report whenever it was required.

Now there are more requirements for storing graphical reports in files so that they can be distributed around an organization as individual pictures, or as part of illustrated reports from word processors or on Web pages, as universal access to SAS software installations is no longer as common. This chapter discusses a number of methods of producing portable graphic report formats using SAS/GRAPH, none of which require SAS/GRAPH software to be installed on the recipient's system.

4.2 Introduction

SAS/GRAPH device drivers are vital links between SAS data and graphics devices and file formats. The device drivers can be listed using PROC GDEVICE, either to the Output window:

```
PROC GDEVICE NOFS;
 LIST _ALL_;
RUN;
```

or in an interactive screen:

```
PROC GDEVICE;
RUN;
```

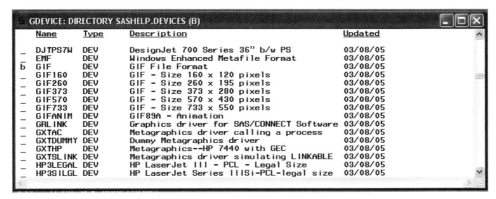

The line command "b" will open the device driver Detail window:

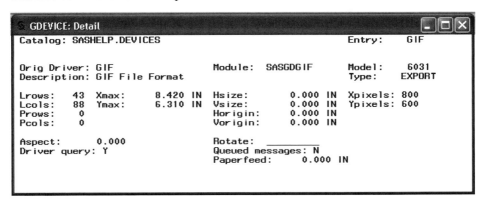

Once the device driver windows have been opened, new menu options are available under **Tools**:

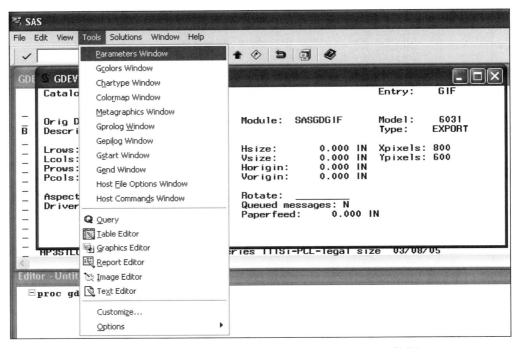

The Parameters window includes details of the maximum colors available:

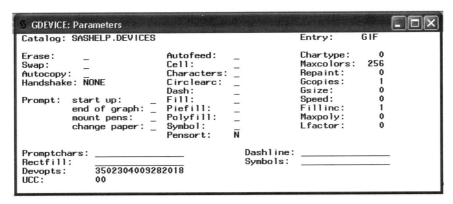

4.3 GIF, JPEG, Bitmap, and Other Graphics File Formats

The bitmap device drivers, e.g., BMP, BMP20, DIB, and SASBMP, produce large image files with no compression, and therefore no data loss.

The Web graphics device drivers, e.g., GIF, GIFANIM, IMGGIF, IMGJPEG, JPEG, and PNG, produce small files with high compression, although with some data loss, which are suitable for Web pages. The specialized Web graphics device drivers ACTXIMG and JAVAIMG create PNG files that look like the images produced by the ACTIVEX and JAVA graphics device drivers (see Section 4.5, "The ACTIVEX and JAVA Graphics Devices"). Note, however, that until SAS 9.2, the JAVAIMG graphics device driver will not create an image when used with a Java Runtime Environment later than 1.4.2.

The vector graphics device drivers, e.g., WMF, SASWMF, EMF, SASEMF, and CGM, are useful primarily as input to word-processing and presentation software, because the images can be resized without loss of detail, and may be optimized for specific applications.

The specialized image device drivers, e.g., HPGL, TIFFP, PDF, PSEPSFA4, and PSLEPSFC, are also designed with specific software in mind, but are based on compressed coded graphics.

All these graphics formats can be generated using standardized SAS/GRAPH code, which was also used to create the file types listed in the summary table at the end of this chapter:

```
%MACRO imagefile(dsn=,device=);
 GOPTIONS RESET=ALL DEVICE=&device
     GSFNAME=newimage GSFMODE=REPLACE;
 FILENAME newimage "&dsn";
 %LET sysrc=%SYSFUNC(FDELETE(newimage));
 PROC GCHART DATA=sashelp.class;
  VBAR age / SUMVAR=weight SUBGROUP=sex DISCRETE;
  TITLE 'VBAR Test Graph';
 RUN;
 QUIT;
```

```
       FILENAME newimage CLEAR;
%MEND;

%imagefile(dsn=g_gif160.gif,device=GIF160)
%imagefile(dsn=g_jpeg.jpg,device=JPEG)
%imagefile(dsn=g_tiffp.tif,device=TIFFP)
%imagefile(dsn=g_pdfc.pdf,device=PDFC)
%imagefile(dsn=g_png.png,device=PNG)
%imagefile(dsn=g_sasbmp.bmp,device=SASBMP)
%imagefile(dsn=g_cgmof971.cgm,device=CGMOF97L)
%imagefile(dsn=g_pslepsfc.eps,device=PSLEPSFC)
%imagefile(dsn=g_wmf.wmf,device=WMF)
```

4.4 The HTML and WEBFRAME Graphics Devices

While the device drivers described in the previous section create individual files for each graph generated, the HTML and WEBFRAME device drivers each create one or more GIF files for each graph and associated HTML files.

The HTML device driver generates a GIF file for each graph and a single HTML output file:

- **index.html** allows you to scroll between the GIF images.

The WEBFRAME device driver creates two GIF files, a thumbnail image and a full-sized image, for each graph generated, two HTML files to control the access and display of the graphs, and an additional HTML file for each full-sized GIF file:

- **index.html** is the master Web page, and contains an HTML frame set comprising an index column and the main image viewing area.

- **sasthumb.html** forms the index column in **index.html**, and holds the thumbnail GIF images of the SAS/GRAPH pictures.

- *graphname*.**html** is the HTML generated for each GIF image from SAS/GRAPH, which is selected to be shown in the main viewing area of **index.html**.

The following sample SAS/GRAPH program demonstrates how the HTML and WEBFRAME device drivers can be used to produce graphical Web-based reports:

```
%MACRO imagehtml(dir=,device=);
  GOPTIONS RESET=ALL DEVICE=&device GSFNAME=imagedir;
  FILENAME imagedir "&dir\device_&device";
  PROC GREPLAY IGOUT=work.gseg NOFS;
   DELETE _ALL_;
  RUN;
  PROC SORT DATA=sashelp.class OUT=work.class;
   BY sex;
  RUN;
  PROC GCHART DATA=work.class;
   BY sex;
   VBAR age / SUMVAR=weight SUBGROUP=name DISCRETE;
   TITLE 'VBAR Test Graph - #BYVAL(sex)';
  RUN;
  QUIT;
  FILENAME imagedir CLEAR;
%MEND;
%imagehtml(dir=g:\web_server\wwwroot\sasweb,device=HTML)
```

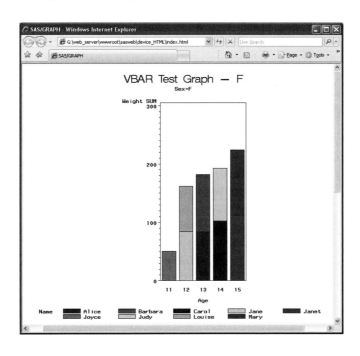

```
%imagehtml(dir=g:\web_server\wwwroot\sasweb,device=WEBFRAME)
```

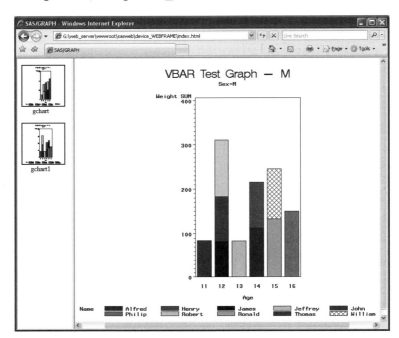

4.5 The ACTIVEX and JAVA Graphics Devices

The HTML and WEBFRAME device drivers cater to static HTML reporting; the ACTIVEX and JAVA device drivers, introduced in SAS 8.2, and JAVA2 device driver introduced in SAS 9, enable the recipient of the report to tailor its appearance by selecting the axes, type of graph, color scheme, and view angle. The user interaction is achieved by the installation of an ActiveX DLL or Java JAR and CLASS files on the user's system prior to receiving the HTML report. The data for the report is stored in JavaScript and HTML parameters in the HTML file, rather than in an image file. The HTML is controlled via ODS HTML statements, which open and close the generated HTML file.

```
%MACRO imageobject(dir=,device=);
 ODS LISTING CLOSE;
 ODS HTML FILE="&dir\&device..html";
 GOPTIONS RESET=ALL DEVICE=&device;
 PROC GCHART DATA=sashelp.class;
  VBAR age / SUMVAR=weight SUBGROUP=sex DISCRETE;
  TITLE "VBAR Test Graph - device=&device";
 RUN;
 QUIT;
 ODS HTML CLOSE;
 ODS LISTING;
%MEND;
%imageobject(dir=g:\web_server\wwwroot\sasweb,device=ACTIVEX)
%imageobject(dir=g:\web_server\wwwroot\sasweb,device=JAVA)
%imageobject(dir=g:\web_server\wwwroot\sasweb,device=JAVA2)
```

There are a number of limitations to the application of the ACTIVEX and JAVA device drivers, even though they can be used with a large number of SAS/GRAPH procedures, including PROC GCHART, PROC GCONTOUR, PROC GMAP, PROC GPLOT, and PROC G3D. If a SAS/GRAPH procedure other than those listed is used, the device driver is overridden by DEVICE=GIF. It should also be noted that no annotation can be added to the graph in SAS 8.2 or SAS 9.1.3, but annotation can be added in SAS 9.2.

4.5.1 SAS/GRAPH ActiveX Control

The ActiveX control that displays the graphical data can be embedded in Web pages (as described previously), Object Linked Embedded (OLE) documents, and applications written in Visual Basic, C++, HTML, and JavaScript. There are a number of features incorporated into the control, including graph reorganization, saving graphs to user files, and drill-down actions, which can be accessed from a floating toolbar. The control is installed in a standard SAS software installation in the folder **C:\Program Files\SAS Institute\Shared Files\Graph**.

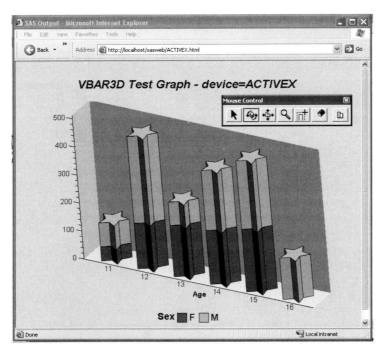

The ActiveX control can be installed automatically on a Web client's system by adding the location of the SASGraph.exe file on the Web server to the report generated by the ACTIVEX device driver. For example:

```
ODS HTML FILE="c:\web_server\wwwroot\sasweb\ACTIVEX.html"
 ATTRIBUTES=("codebase"=
        "http://web_server/controls/SASGraph.exe");
GOPTIONS RESET=ALL DEVICE=ACTIVEX;
```

This CODEBASE= attribute enables the HTML file to start the installation program if the SAS/GRAPH ActiveX control is not yet installed on the web client's system. It should be noted that the installation will take place only when the user accepts the licensing agreement that is displayed at the beginning of the installation process.

4.5.2 SAS/GRAPH Java Applets

The Java applets used to display the graphical data provide a number of features, including graph reorganization, saving graphs to user files, and drill-down actions, which can be accessed from a floating toolbar, by clicking the Graph Toolbar option, but only if the graph is 3D and has three axes defined. The applets are installed in a standard SAS software installation in the folder **C:\Program Files\SAS\Shared Files\Applets** if SAS 8 is not installed, or in **C:\Program Files\SAS Institute\Shared Files\Applets** if SAS 8 is installed, and they require a Java Runtime Environment and Web browser to be installed that will support Java 1.1.4 or later. The applets will also work if Java 1.5 is installed.

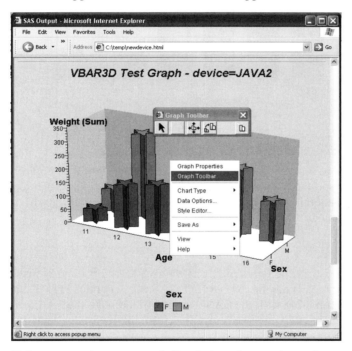

If there are only two axes defined, then the graph can be customized, but not rotated. The JAVA and JAVA2 device drivers will generate the same images.

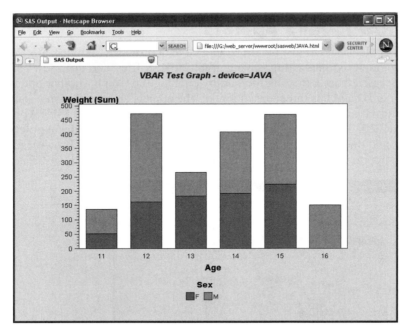

For all Web clients to be able to access these applets, they should be copied to a folder on the Web server and the SAS system option APPLETLOC= set to that location, so that programs used to generate HTML files using the JAVA device driver will include this location. For example:

```
OPTIONS APPLETLOC="http://web_server/applets";
```

Caution: If SAS 9 is installed on a platform where SAS 8.2 is already installed, the Java applets can be overwritten. SAS 8.2 generates HTML that is not compatible with the SAS 9 applets. To restore the SAS 8.2 Java applets, they must be reinstalled from the SAS 8.2 Client-Side Components CD-ROM.

4.6 The SAS Metagraphics Data Devices

In addition to the JAVA device driver, there are three other device drivers, also introduced in SAS 8.2, that generate special SAS metagraphics data suitable for input into the MetaViewApplet Java applet in the **METAFILE.ZIP** file, which can also be found in the Applets folder:

- **SASMETA** uses the GOPTIONS parameter GSFNAME= to specify the destination of any SAS metagraphics data file generated.

```
FILENAME imgdata "c:\web_server\graph\meta.txt";
%LET sysrc=%SYSFUNC(FDELETE(imgdata));
GOPTIONS RESET=ALL DEVICE=SASMETA GSFNAME=imgdata;
... more SAS/GRAPH code ... *;
FILENAME imgdata CLEAR;
```

- **JAVAMETA** (experimental in SAS 8.2) writes the SAS metagraphics data to a file associated with the _WEBOUT file reference. It includes 33 scalable fonts.

```
FILENAME _webout "c:\web_server\graph\meta.txt";
%LET sysrc=%SYSFUNC(FDELETE(_webout));
GOPTIONS RESET=ALL DEVICE=JAVAMETA;
... more SAS/GRAPH code ... *;
FILENAME _webout CLEAR;
```

- **JAVAPUB** (experimental in SAS 8.2) is coded like the SASMETA device driver, but creates SAS metagraphics data identical to that of the JAVAMETA device driver. It also includes 33 scalable fonts.

```
FILENAME imgdata "c:\web_server\graph\meta.txt";
%LET sysrc=%SYSFUNC(FDELETE(imgdata));
GOPTIONS RESET=ALL DEVICE=JAVAPUB GSFNAME=imgdata;
... more SAS/GRAPH code ... *;
FILENAME imgdata CLEAR;
```

All these device drivers can create SAS metagraphics data from any SAS/GRAPH procedure, graphic annotation, and DSGI (DATA Step Graphics Interface) graphic. The MetaViewApplet incorporates a number of features, including graph resizing, scrolling using embedded controls, animated scrolling in the form of a slide show presentation, drill-down to other graphs without loading a new HTML page, and display of data tips in response to moving the mouse over events.

Graphical report development for the Web using the SASMETA, JAVAMETA, or JAVAPUB device drivers and the MetaViewApplet requires two programming steps:

1. Use a SAS/GRAPH program, or DSGI, with the device driver to generate GIF files based on metagraphics codes.

2. Create an HTML file on a Web server to display the GIF images.

There are four choices for creating the HTML file on the Web server, which are illustrated in the following examples:

- Create the HTML file outside of SAS.

```
<HTML>
<HEAD>
<TITLE>Example HTML File</TITLE>
</HEAD>
<BODY>
<APPLET CODEBASE="http://web_server/applets"
        ARCHIVE="metafile.zip"
        CODE="MetaViewApplet.class"
        WIDTH="640"
        HEIGHT="480"
        ALIGN="TOP">
    <PARAM NAME="BackgroundColor" VALUE="0xffffff">
    <PARAM NAME="Metacodes"
        VALUE="http://web_server/graph/meta.txt">
    Sorry, your browser does not support the APPLET tag.
</APPLET>
</BODY>
</HTML>
```

- Create the HTML file using PUT statements in your SAS program.

```
FILENAME outfile "c:\web_server\graph\sashtml.htm";
  DATA _NULL_;
    LENGTH codebase archive parent $100;
    codebase=QUOTE("http://web_server/applets");
    archive=QUOTE("metafile.zip");
    parent=QUOTE("http://web_server/graph/meta.txt");
    FILE outfile;
    PUT '<HTML>';
    PUT '<HEAD>';
    PUT '<TITLE>Example HTML file</title>';
    PUT '</HEAD>';
    PUT '<BODY>';
    PUT '<APPLET ARCHIVE=' archive;
    PUT '  CODEBASE=' codebase;
    PUT '  CODE="MetaViewApplet.class"';
```

```
              PUT '  WIDTH="640" HEIGHT="480" ALIGN="TOP">';
              PUT '  <PARAM NAME="ZoomControlEnabled" VALUE="false">';
              PUT '  <PARAM NAME="BackgroundColor" VALUE="0xffffff">';
              PUT '  <PARAM NAME="Metacodes" VALUE=' parent '>';
              PUT '</APPLET>';
              PUT '</BODY>';
              PUT '</HTML>';
RUN;
FILENAME outfile CLEAR;
```

- Use the META2HTM macro, which is supplied as part of the SAS/GRAPH
  component installation, in your SAS program.

```
FILENAME _webout "c:\web_server\graph\meta2htm.htm";
%META2HTM(capture=on,
     htmlfref=_webout,
     openmode=REPLACE,
     codebase=http://web_server/applets,
     archive=metafile.zip);
GOPTIONS RESET=ALL DEVICE=JAVAMETA;
... more SAS/GRAPH code ... *;
%META2HTM(capture=off,
     htmlfref=_webout,
     openmode=APPEND);
FILENAME _webout CLEAR;
```

- Use the Output Delivery System in your SAS program to create the HTML file.

```
FILENAME odsout "c:\web_server\graph";
GOPTIONS RESET=ALL DEVICE=JAVAMETA;
ODS LISTING CLOSE;
ODS HTML FILE='ods.htm' PATH=odsout;
... more SAS/GRAPH code ... *;
ODS HTML CLOSE;
ODS LISTING;
```

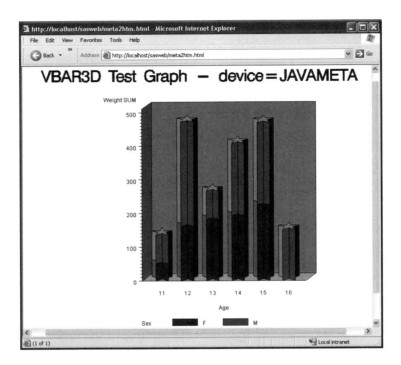

4.7 Creating Drill-Down Graphs

Static graphical reports with single images, as we have been discussing so far, have more limited use than reports where additional information can be displayed, if requested. These drill-down reports can be generated using a number of different device drivers, representing the additional information as extra files, or as extended data stored within the HTML of the main Web page.

4.7.1 HTML and WEBFRAME Device Drivers

Because the HTML and WEBFRAME device drivers always overwrite the **index.html** file that is used as the main Web page for any report, the output files should be placed in their own folders. These device drivers also will not assign anchor names within the generated HTML in the output files. These features restrict the usefulness of these device drivers for drill-down reports, so they are really practical only to drill down to GIF image files, and not to HTML files containing multiple pieces of output. It is easier to use ODS to generate drill-down graphs in this situation.

However, for the HTML and WEBFRAME device drivers, the drill-down capabilities are activated by the use of the IMAGEMAP= option, and a variable in the input data that should hold information to link it to drill-down images, which is referred to by the HTML= option.

```
/* This is the only line you have to change to run the
   program. Specify a location in your file system. */
FILENAME out 'c:\web_server\wwwroot\sasweb\HTML-drill';
/* assign graphics options for ODS output */
GOPTIONS XPIXELS=480 YPIXELS=400 GSFNAME=out DEVICE=HTML;
OPTIONS NOBYLINE;
/* create data set REGSALES */
DATA regsales;
 SET sashelp.prdsale;
 LENGTH links $40; /* the HTML variable */
 /* add the HTML variable and assign its values */
 IF country='CANADA' THEN links='href="salereg1.gif"';
 ELSE IF country='GERMANY' THEN links='href="salereg2.gif"';
 ELSE IF country='U.S.A.' THEN links='href="salereg3.gif"';
RUN;
PROC GCHART DATA=regsales IMAGEMAP=salemap;
 VBAR3D country / SUMVAR=actual PATTERNID=midpoint
         HTML=links NAME='htmldril';
 TITLE1 'Company Sales';
RUN;
/* change to GIF driver for pie charts */
GOPTIONS DEVICE=GIF;
PROC SORT DATA=regsales OUT=regsales;
 BY country;
RUN;
/* Create three charts that use the HTML variable */
PROC GCHART DATA=regsales;
 DONUT product / SUMVAR=actual NOHEADING SLICE=OUTSIDE
         PERCENT=INSIDE VALUE=INSIDE NAME='salereg1';
 BY country;
 TITLE2 'Product Sales for #BYVAL(country)';
RUN;
QUIT;
FILENAME out CLEAR;
```

This example uses the HTML device driver; the principles also apply to the WEBFRAME device driver. The drill-down occurs when a section of the main image is clicked.

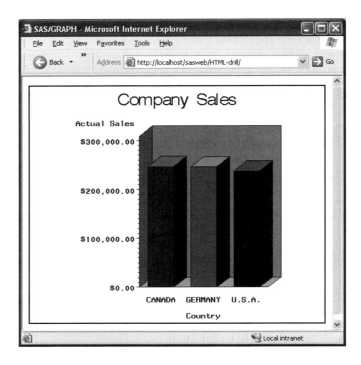

The Back button on the Web browser can be used to return from the drill-down image to the main Web page.

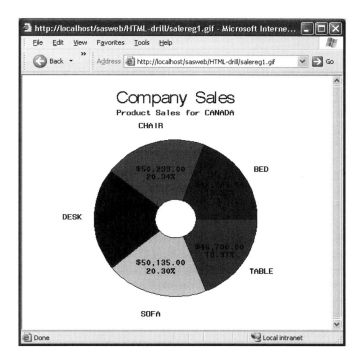

4.7.2 SAS Metagraphics Data Device Drivers

No HTML is generated directly by the SAS metagraphics device drivers, so the HTML must be written separately, or generated using ODS or the META2HTM macro.

The individual images are stored as text files when the HTML is generated separately, which means that the Web data loaded by the Web browser is related only to the images viewed. This method should be preferred only when a small proportion of the images are likely to be viewed in any particular session. As with the HTML and WEBFRAME device drivers, the IMAGEMAP= and HTML= options are used to direct the drill-down action to the corresponding drill-down image.

```
<html>
<head>
</head>
<body>
<applet archive="metafile.zip"
  codebase="./applets"
  code="MetaViewApplet.class"
  width="640" height="480" align="TOP">
  <param name="ZoomControlEnabled" value="flase">
  <param name="BackgroundColor" value="0xffffff">
  <param name="Metacodes" value="javameta_html_allyears.txt" >
</applet>
</body>
</html>
```

All of the SAS metagraphics data created when the HTML is generated using ODS, or the META2HTM macro, is actually included in the HTML file itself, which means that the data for the entire image collection must be loaded when the main Web page is opened. The response times for drill-down image loading will be much faster than for the previous method with separately generated HTML, but will be much slower to load the main Web page with the first image. Note that the IMAGEMAP= option is not required in this case, but the HTML= option is still needed to provide information to link this image to the appropriate drill-down image.

```
/* Create a macro variable to simplify substitution */
%LET codepath=./applets;
%LET filepath=g:\web_server\wwwroot\sasweb;
/* Create a new HTML file*/
FILENAME outfile "&filepath\javameta_html.html";
DATA _null_;
 LENGTH codebase archive parent $100;
 codebase=QUOTE("&codepath");
 archive=QUOTE("metafile.zip");
 parent= QUOTE("javameta_html_allyears.txt");
 FILE outfile;
 PUT '<html>';
 PUT '<head>';
 PUT '</head>';
 PUT '<body>';
 PUT '<applet archive=' archive;
 PUT '  codebase=' codebase;
 PUT '  code="MetaViewApplet.class"';
 PUT '  width="640" height="480" align="TOP">';
 PUT '  <param name="ZoomControlEnabled" value="false">';
 PUT '  <param name="BackgroundColor" value="0xffffff">';
 PUT '  <param name="Metacodes" value=' parent '>';
 PUT '</applet>';
```

```
 PUT '</body>';
 PUT '</html>';
RUN;
/* Deassign fileref */
FILENAME outfile;
/* Summarize the data by YEAR, QUARTER and YEAR*QUARTER */
PROC SUMMARY DATA=sashelp.prdsale;
 CLASS year quarter;
 VAR actual;
 OUTPUT OUT=prdsummary SUM=actual;
RUN;
/* Post-process the summarized data to create the HTML variable
   holding the text for the drill-down. */
DATA yearsonly;
 SET prdsummary(WHERE=(_TYPE_ EQ 2));
 LENGTH htmlvar $600 menustring $100;
 /* MENU= defines pop-up menu text and actions */
 menustring='menu=['||
        QUOTE('1993 by Quarter')||'= '||
        QUOTE('1994 by Quarter')||'=]';
 /* MREF= defines the file of metacodes for drill-down actions
*/
 htmlvar='mref='||QUOTE("javameta_html_y"||PUT(year,4.)||
      '.txt')||' '||menustring;
RUN;
/* Use JAVAMETA device driver to create graphics metadata */
goptions RESET=ALL DEV=JAVAMETA
      COLORS=(blue yellow red cyan) CTEXT=black
      FTEXT="Helvetica" FTITLE="Helvetica"
      HTEXT=24 PT HTITLE=32 PT ;
/* Assign _WEBOUT. Remove any earlier version. */
FILENAME _webout "&filepath\javameta_html_allyears.txt";
%LET sysrc=%SYSFUNC(FDELETE(_webout));
/* The IMAGEMAP= and HTML= options add the MREF= and MENU=
values
   to the metagraphics data */
TITLE1 '1993-1994 Sales';
PROC GCHART DATA=yearsonly IMAGEMAP=temp ;
 PIE year / SUMVAR=actual DISCRETE NOLEGEND VALUE=ARROW
        SLICE=ARROW HTML=htmlvar;
RUN;
QUIT;
```

```
/* Assign _WEBOUT to a drill-down file.
   Remove any earlier version */
FILENAME _webout "&filepath\javameta_html_y1993.txt";
%LET sysrc=%SYSFUNC(FDELETE(_webout));
TITLE1 '1993 Quarterly Sales';
GOPTIONS COLORS=(red cyan tan ltgray);
PROC GCHART DATA=prdsummary (WHERE=(YEAR EQ 1993 AND _TYPE_ EQ
3));
   PIE quarter / SUMVAR=actual DISCRETE NOLEGEND
         VALUE=ARROW SLICE=ARROW;
RUN;
QUIT;
/* Assign _WEBOUT to a drill-down file.
   Remove any earlier version */
FILENAME _webout "&filepath\javameta_html_y1994.txt";
%LET sysrc=%SYSFUNC(FDELETE(_webout));
GOPTIONS COLORS=(red cyan tan ltgray);
TITLE1 '1994 Quarterly Sales';
PROC GCHART DATA=prdsummary (WHERE=(year EQ 1994 AND _TYPE_ EQ
3));
   PIE quarter / sumvar=actual DISCRETE NOLEGEND
         VALUE=ARROW SLICE=ARROW;
RUN;
QUIT;
/* Deassign fileref */
FILENAME _webout
```

This example uses the JAVAMETA device driver; the principles also apply to the SASMETA and JAVAPUB device drivers. The drill-down occurs when a section of the main image is clicked.

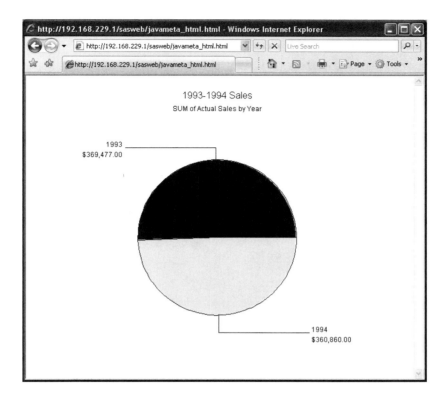

The Back option on the pop-up menu that appears when you right-click the image on the Web page can be used to return from the drill-down image to the main Web page. Once the main Web page is redisplayed, the Forward option is added to the pop-up menu for that image. It should be noted that the Web address shown remains unchanged throughout the drill-down actions, so the Back button on the Web browser cannot be used to return to the main Web page.

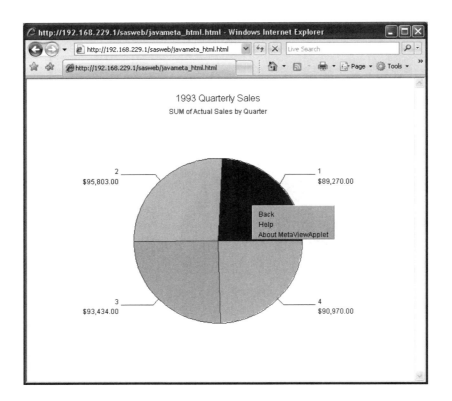

4.8 Summary

The following list of device drivers with TYPE=EXPORT in SAS 8.2 (†), SAS 9.1.3 (*), or both, shows their color capabilities and the software that can read that format (0=incompatible, and 1=poor to 6=very good).

Table 4.1 List of Device Drivers with TYPE=EXPORT

Device Driver	Kb	MSO 2000: W[6]	MSO 2000: XL	MSO 2000: PP	LSS 9.5: WP	LSS 9.5: 123	LSS 9.5: FG	OOo 2.1: Wr	OOo 2.1: Ca	OOo 2.1: Im	OOo 2.1: Dr	Web: IE	Web: NS	Edit: Paint
ACTXIMG*	1	5	5	5	5	0	0	5	5	5	5	5	5	5
BMP	2120	5	5	5	4	5	4	5	5	5	5	0	0	5
BMP20	2120	5	5	5	4	4	4	5	5	5	5	0	0	5
CGM	2	4	3	3	2	2	2	0	0	3	0	0	0	0
CGM123C†	18	5	5	5	5	5	5	0	0	3	0	0	0	0
CGMAM3C†	18	5	5	5	5	5	5	0	0	3	0	0	0	0
CGMAPSA†	2	5	5	5	5	5	5	0	0	3	0	0	0	0
CGMC	4	4	4	4	2	2	2	0	0	3	0	0	0	0
CGMCHAR	2	0	0	0	0	0	0	0	0	0	0	0	0	0
CGMCLEAR	4	4	4	3	2	2	2	0	0	0	0	0	0	0
CGMCRT†	1	2	2	2	2	2	2	0	0	3	0	0	0	0
CGMCRTCH†	1	0	0	0	0	0	0	0	0	0	0	0	0	0
CGMCRTCL†	1	2	2	2	2	2	2	0	0	0	0	0	0	0
CGMFL2C†	18	5	5	5	5	5	5	0	0	3	0	0	0	0
CGMFLM†	1	4	3	3	2	2	2	0	0	3	0	0	0	0
CGMFLWA†	2	5	5	5	5	5	5	0	0	3	0	0	0	0
CGMHG3A†	5	2	2	2	5	5	5	0	0	3	0	0	0	0
CGMHGWA†	2	5	5	5	5	5	5	0	0	3	0	0	0	0
CGMILFC†	18	5	5	5	5	5	5	0	0	3	0	0	0	0
CGMLT97L	3	5	5	5	5	5	5	0	0	3	0	0	0	0
CGMLT97P	3	5	5	5	5	5	5	0	0	3	0	0	0	0
CGMMPPA†	2	5	5	5	5	5	5	0	0	3	0	0	0	0
CGMMW6C†	14	5	5	5	5	5	5	0	0	3	0	0	0	0
CGMOF97L	4	5	5	5	5	5	5	0	0	3	0	0	0	0
CGMOF97P	3	5	5	5	5	5	5	0	0	3	0	0	0	0
CGMOFML*	36	5	5	5	5	5	5	0	0	3	0	0	0	0

Table 4.1 (*continued*)

Device Driver	Kb	MSO 2000: W[6]	MSO 2000: XL	MSO 2000: PP	LSS 9.5: WP	LSS 9.5: 123	LSS 9.5: FG	OOo 2.1: Wr	OOo 2.1: Ca	OOo 2.1: Im	OOo 2.1: Dr	Web: IE	Web: NS	Edit: Paint
CGMOFMP*	30	5	5	5	5	5	5	0	0	3	0	0	0	0
CGMWP†	10	5	5	5	2	2	2	0	0	3	0	0	0	0
CGMWP61L†	1	5	5	5	5	5	5	0	0	3	0	0	0	0
CGMWP61P†	1	5	5	5	5	5	5	0	0	3	0	0	0	0
CGMWP80L†	3	5	5	5	5	5	5	0	0	3	0	0	0	0
CGMWP80P†	3	5	5	5	5	5	5	0	0	3	0	0	0	0
CGMWPCA†	2	5	5	5	5	5	5	0	0	3	0	0	0	0
CGMWPCAP†	2	5	5	5	5	5	5	0	0	3	0	0	0	0
CGMWPL†	10	5	5	5	3	3	3	0	0	3	0	0	0	0
CGMWPWA†	16	5	5	5	5	5	5	0	0	3	0	0	0	0
DIB	2120	5	5	5	5	5	5	5	5	5	5	0	0	5
EMF	4	3	4	3	5	0	0	3	5	4	4	0	0	5
GIF	1	5	5	5	5	5	5	5	5	5	5	5	5	5
GIF160	1	1	1	1	1	1	1	1	1	1	1	5	5	1
GIF260	1	3	3	3	2	2	2	2	2	2	2	5	5	2
GIF373	1	4	4	4	4	4	4	4	4	4	4	5	5	4
GIF570	1	5	5	5	5	5	5	5	5	5	5	5	5	5
GIF733	1	5	5	5	5	5	5	5	5	5	5	5	5	5
GIFANIM	9	5	5	5	4	4	4	5	5	5	5	5	5	0
HPGL	7	0	0	0	5	0	0	0	0	0	0	0	0	0
IMGGIF†	1	5	5	5	5	5	5	5	5	5	5	5	5	5
IMGJPEG†	2	5	5	5	5	5	5	5	5	5	5	5	5	5
IMGPBM†	3	0	0	0	0	0	0	5	5	5	5	0	0	0
IMGPPM†	61	0	0	0	0	0	0	5	5	5	5	0	0	0
JAVAIMG*	1	5	5	5	5	0	0	5	5	5	5	5	5	5

Table 4.1 (*continued*)

Device Driver	Kb	MSO 2000: W[6]	MSO 2000: XL	MSO 2000: PP	LSS 9.5: WP	LSS 9.5: 123	LSS 9.5: FG	OOo 2.1: Wr	OOo 2.1: Ca	OOo 2.1: Im	OOo 2.1: Dr	Web: IE	Web: NS	Edit: Paint
JPEG	2	5	5	5	5	5	5	5	5	5	5	5	5	5
PDF	6	0	0	0	0	0	0	0	0	0	0	5[4]	5[4]	0
PDFC	2	0	0	0	0	0	0	0	0	0	0	5[4]	5[4]	0
PNG	1	5	5	5	5	0	0	5	5	5	5	5	5	0
PSEPSF	2	1	1	1	1	0	0	0	0	0	0	0	0	0
PSEPSFA4	2	1	1	1	1	0	0	0	0	0	0	0	0	0
PSLEPSF	2	1	1	1	1	0	0	0	0	0	0	0	0	0
PSLEPSFC	2	1	1	1	1	0	0	0	0	0	0	0	0	0
SASBMP	2	5	5	5	5	5	5	5	5	5	5	0	0	5
SASEMF	5	5	5	5	5	0	0	5	5	5	5	0	0	5
SASWMF	3	5	5	5	5	5	5	5	5	5	5	0	0	3
TIFFB	1	5	5	5	5	0	5	5	5	5	5	0	0	5
TIFFBII	1	5	5	5	5	0	5	5	5	5	5	0	0	5
TIFFBMM	1	5	5	5	5	0	5	5	5	5	5	0	0	5
TIFFG3†	1	5	5	5	0	0	5	5	5	5	5	0	0	5
TIFFG4†	7	5	5	5	0	0	5	5	5	5	5	0	0	5
TIFFP	2	5	5	5	5	0	5	5	5	5	5	0	0	5
WMF	2	2	5	3	3	3	5	2	1	4	3	0	0	5

Device Driver	Kb	MSO 2000: W[6]	MSO 2000: XL	MSO 2000: PP	LSS 9.5: WP	OOo 2.1: Wr	Web: IE	Web: NS
HTML	[2]	5[2]	3[2]	5[2]	0[2]	0[2]	5[2]	5[2]
WEBFRAME	[3]	5[3]	0[3]	0[3]	0[3]	0[3]	5[3]	5[3]

Table 4.1 (*continued*)

Device Driver	Kb	Web: IE	Web: NS
ACTIVEX	(1)	5[1]	5[1]
JAVA	(1)	5[1]	5[1]
JAVA2*	(1)	5[1]	5[1]

Device Driver	Kb	OOo 2.1: Wr	Web: IE	Web: NS
JAVAMETA	2	5[5]	5[1]	5[1]
JAVAPUB	2	5[5]	5[1]	5[1]
SASMETA	2	5[5]	5[1]	5[1]

Notes:

1. The ACTIVEX, JAVA, JAVA2, JAVAMETA, JAVAPUB, and SASMETA device drivers generate parameterized HTML for preinstalled ActiveX DLL or Java JAR files, when used with ODS HTML statements.

2. The HTML device driver generates individual GIF and HTML files to create scrolling graphs.

3. The WEBFRAME device driver generates multiple GIF and HTML files to create an indexed collection of images.

4. PDF and PDFC device drivers require Acrobat Reader plug-ins for Web browsers to display files.

5. Only HTML files, with instream metagraphics data, generated by ODS, are compatible.

6. MSO=Microsoft Office, LSS=Lotus SmartSuite, OOo=OpenOffice.org/StarOffice, W=Word, XL=Excel, PP=PowerPoint, WP=Word Pro, 123=1-2-3, FG=Freelance Graphics, Wr=Writer, Ca=Calc, Im=Impress, Dr=Draw, IE=Internet Explorer, NS=Netscape/Firefox.

4.9 Recommended Reading

For more information, go to
www.hollandnumerics.com/books/Saving_Time_and_Money_using_SAS.htm. This
page includes a chapter-by-chapter list of recommended reading.

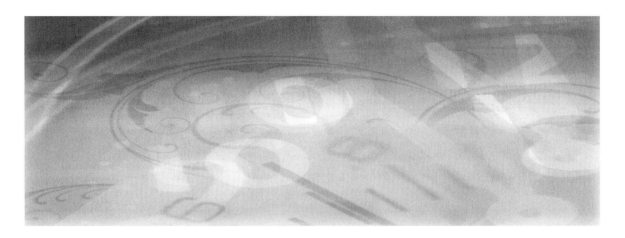

Chapter **5**

Importing Data from and Exporting Data to Databases without SAS/ACCESS

5.1 Abstract

This chapter discusses a number of methods of importing data from and exporting data to external databases and spreadsheets using SAS software without the need to license SAS/ACCESS software. It also looks at techniques for reading specific data types, e.g., EBCDIC characters, packed and zoned decimals, dates and times, etc., from flat files into SAS data sets.

5.2 Introduction

SAS/ACCESS software is configured for specific database systems, e.g., DB2, Oracle, ODBC, etc., which must be licensed separately. The software enables SAS to read data held in a database as if it were in SAS data sets, or directly through native database SQL. The software uses the power of the database system, which is its strength and its weakness. The strength lies in the use of the database's internal systems to make the external interface to SAS very consistent, no matter which database system is being accessed. The weakness lies in the performance impact the SAS/ACCESS software has on the database system while the database data is being accessed. It is this weakness that this chapter addresses.

5.3 Access to Live Database Data

No self-respecting database administrator should ever allow unregulated access to live data available to SAS/ACCESS software users, particularly if the database is being used to support transaction-based processing. The performance impact on live production systems can be dramatic if a long-running query is started. Response times of production transactions can greatly increase as the processing resources become scarcer due to other processes taking away more and more.

The usual alternative is to create a copy of the database at set intervals to provide a regularly updated snapshot of the live database for querying by SAS/ACCESS. This database copy would still need to be maintained by the database administrators to make certain the query performance is acceptable, without adversely affecting the performance of the production systems.

Figure 5.1 Options for Copying Data from Live Databases into SAS

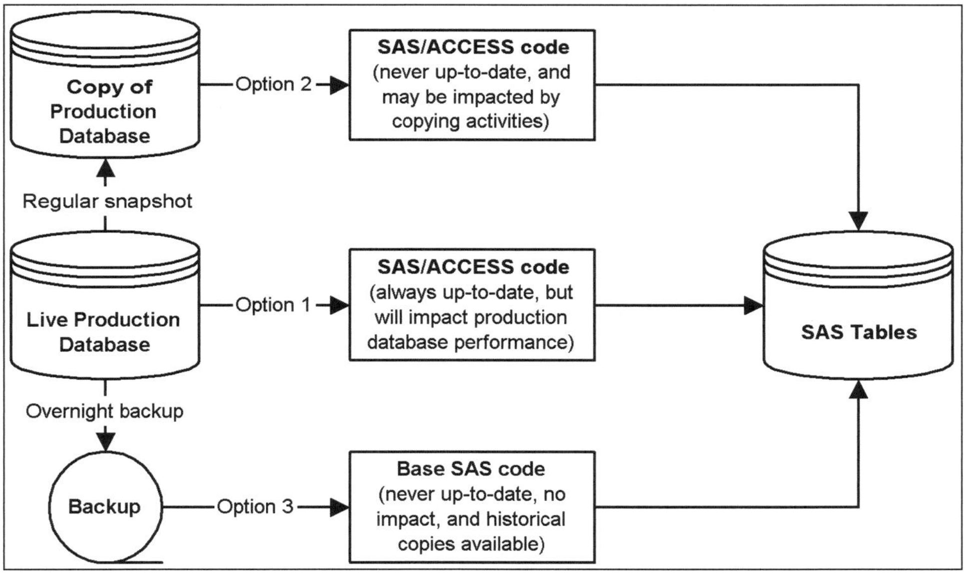

5.4 Access to Database Extracts

Although creating extracts of production databases appears to be generating extra work for the database administrators, it is very likely that suitable extracts are already being created on a regular basis as part of the automated backup processing. These backup files are usually flat files containing the data stored in database records as delimited or fixed column files.

The following sections describe the techniques used to copy data from these backup files into SAS data sets, which can then be queried using your available SAS components.

5.4.1 Delimited Flat Files

Comma-separated files contain rows of data items with each item separated from the next by a comma. Character data items can also be optionally surrounded by quotation marks, which is vital if the data items contain commas. The INFILE statement must specify the separator using the DLM= (or DELIMITER=) option. The DSD option is also recommended if missing data items could be indicated by adjacent commas. Note that the DSD option sets the default delimiter comma, so the DLM= option is only required to change the delimiter, e.g., to tab.

The following examples use the TRUNCOVER option, which will save the contents of partially filled variables at the end of an input record. The MISSOVER option would save a missing value in the same situation.

Use the TRUNCOVER option (my own preference) under the following conditions:

- when the input record has a variable length, and trailing blanks may not be present
- when the record length (LRECL= and LINESIZE=) is sufficient to include the entire records
- when any data, even if less than the full variable length, is acceptable

Use the MISSOVER option under the following conditions:

- when the input record has a fixed length
- when warnings need to be issued if the INPUT statement has been coded too long for the actual input record length
- when missing values are acceptable for partially filled variables at the end of an input record

```
* Comma-separated text file *;
INFILE 'data.csv' DSD TRUNCOVER LRECL=1024;
```

Tab-separated files differ from comma-separated files only by the separator itself. The tab character can be represented only by hexadecimal notation, which is different for z/OS and the other platforms, so the INFILE statement has to be written specifically for the data source.

```
* Tab-separated text file in EBCDIC *;
INFILE 'zos.txt' DLM='05'x DSD TRUNCOVER LRECL=1024;

* Tab-separated text file in ASCII *;
INFILE 'ascii.txt' DLM='09'x DSD TRUNCOVER LRECL=1024;
```

Having described the input data, you will now need to specify the names and data types of every item in the record, in the correct order. The extract may have the names of the items in the first row of the delimited file, which must be skipped if you intend to read in only the data records.

```
DATA work.csvdata;
  * Comma-separated text file *;
  INFILE 'data.csv' DSD TRUNCOVER LRECL=500 FIRSTOBS=2;
  INFORMAT name $8. sex $1. age weight height BEST32.;
  INPUT name $ age sex $ weight height;
RUN;
```

There is an alternative, if you are using OpenVMS, OS/2, Linux, UNIX, or Windows, and you are prepared to trust SAS to select the correct data type from scanning your data records, and the names of the items are in the first row of the extract, it may be practical to use PROC IMPORT instead. You should use DBMS=CSV for comma-separated files, DBMS=TAB for tab-separated files, or DBMS=DLM for general delimited files. Note also that PROC IMPORT will not replace a table unless instructed to do so.

```
* Comma-separated text file *;
PROC IMPORT DATAFILE='data.csv' DBMS=DLM OUT=work.csvdata
REPLACE;
  DELIMITER=',';
  GETNAMES=YES;
  DATAROW=2;
RUN;
```

The generated SAS DATA step code is then displayed in the SAS log, as well as the preceding PROC IMPORT code.

However, problems may result from the use of PROC IMPORT when the width and/or type of data varies significantly through the delimited file. If the early records have shorter values than later records, or the early records have numeric values, but the later records have character values, then the later records may be read into the SAS data set as truncated or even missing values. The only solution is to somehow force the longest character fields to be read first, which will force the resulting SAS field to be a character variable with sufficient width to accommodate all the subsequent data, either by concatenating the delimited file with a known header file, or prepending a suitable record:

```
DATA _NULL_;
  * Comma-separated text file *;
  INFILE 'data.csv';
  FILE 'data_new.csv';
  * Generate a 'header' record with dummy text values
    of sufficient width *;
  LENGTH field_text $50;
  width = 50;
  field_count = 20;
  field_text = REPEAT('?', width);
  IF _N_ = 1 THEN DO;
    PUT '"' field_text +(-1) '"' @;
    IF field_count > 1 THEN DO i=2 TO field_count;
      PUT ',"' field_text +(-1) '"' @;
    END;
    PUT ' ';
  END;
  * Read in the records from the CSV file *;
  INPUT;
  PUT _INFILE_;
RUN;
* The resulting updated CSV file can now be imported into SAS
*;
```

SAS/ACCESS for PC Files (formerly SAS/ACCESS for PC File Formats) can be used to read spreadsheet files from certain releases of a number of spreadsheet applications. However, all releases of all spreadsheet applications can save spreadsheet data as comma-separated, or other delimited, files, which can be read in the same way as the delimited extract files from databases.

5.4.2 Fixed-Column Data

Not all extracted data can be written into delimited files. In particular, where the data could potentially have bytes representing any of the 256 character codes, there would be no delimiter that could be used. With no possible delimiting of data items by specific characters, the only other option is to begin and end data items at fixed positions across the record, with each range being filled to a known data layout. This is fixed-column data, which means that the records are also likely to be fixed length. An example of DATA step code to read a fixed-column data extract looks like the following:

```
DATA work.fixedcolumn;
  * Fixed-column data file *;
  INFILE 'fixed.dat' TRUNCOVER LRECL=33;
  INFORMAT name $8. sex $1. age weight height 8.;
  INPUT @1 name $ @9 sex $ @10 age @18 weight @26 height;
RUN;
```

If you want to check that the numeric input data is being read correctly, you could reread the numeric data items into character items. These values can then be scrutinized if missing values occur in the numeric items. This is often caused by an incorrect starting location being coded for a data item. It is always a good idea to map out the locations of the start of the individual data columns, which will prevent errors of this type, before writing the INPUT statement.

```
DATA work.fixedcolumn2;
  * Fixed-column data file *;
  INFILE 'fixed.dat' TRUNCOVER LRECL=33;
  INFORMAT name $8. sex $1. age weight height 8.
        age_char weight_char height_char $8.;
  INPUT @1 name $ @9 sex $ @10 age @18 weight @26 height
        @10 age_char $ @18 weight_char $ @26 height_char $;
RUN;
```

5.4.3 Fixed-Block Data

So far I have been assuming that the extract file has data organized as separate records, so that they can be read in using the option LRECL=*nnn*, where *nnn* is greater than or equal to, the maximum record length. Quite often data stored as fixed-column data is also stored in fixed-block files, so that there are no separators between records, and the record number has to be determined by counting record lengths. As such, the data is a continuous stream with only a logical record structure, so the LRECL= parameter must be set to the exact length of the record data. The RECFM=F parameter is used to indicate that the data has fixed record lengths.

```
DATA work.fixedblock;
  * Fixed-column fixed-block data file *;
  INFILE 'fixedblk.dat' TRUNCOVER RECFM=F LRECL=33;
  INFORMAT name $8. sex $1. age weight height 8.
        age_char weight_char height_char $8.;
  INPUT @1 name $ @9 sex $ @10 age @18 weight @26 height
        @10 age_char $ @18 weight_char $ @26 height_char $;
RUN;
```

5.4.4 **Reading All Data as Text**

As I mentioned earlier when describing the reading of fixed-column data, invalid data values could be present in the data. The invalid numeric data will be stored as missing values, and the cause will be difficult to identify, particularly if there are also valid missing values as well. The log may provide some information that could help identify the causes of the unexpected missing values. However, if the number of records with errors exceeds the maximum number of errors that can be displayed (by default this is only 20 records, but can be changed using OPTIONS ERRORS=*n*, where *n* is the maximum number of error messages that will be displayed for each program step), then you may never see all the causes in the first pass through the data.

```
data test;
  input a b c d e;
  list;
  datalines;
1  2  3  4  5
2  3  a  5  6
3  4  5  b  7
run;
```

Even so, this information in the log can be a valuable clue to resolving data issues:

```
1      data test;
2        input a b c d e;
3        list;
4        datalines;

RULE:     ----+----1----+----2----+----3----+----4----+----5----+
5              1  2  3  4  5
NOTE: Invalid data for c in line 6 7-7.
6              2  3  a  5  6
a=2 b=3 c=. d=5 e=6 _ERROR_=1 _N_=2
NOTE: Invalid data for d in line 7 10-10.
7              3  4  5  b  7
a=3 b=4 c=5 d=. e=7 _ERROR_=1 _N_=3
NOTE: The data set WORK.TEST has 3 observations and 5
      variables.
```

Earlier I suggested rereading the numeric data into corresponding character items, which could be scrutinized later. This technique is probably better generalized and automated, if there are large quantities of data being read into SAS data sets, by initially reading all the data into character items, before testing, converting, and copying the numeric values into the correct numeric items, while reporting any problems.

```
DATA work.charin (KEEP=name sex age weight height)
    work.errors (KEEP=name sex flag
                        age_char weight_char height_char);
  * Fixed-column data file with a mixture of numbers and text
*;
  INFILE 'mixed.dat' TRUNCOVER LRECL=33;
  INFORMAT name $8. sex $1.
          age_char weight_char height_char $8.;
  flag=0;
  INPUT @1 name $ @9 sex $
        @10 age_char $ @18 weight_char $ @26 height_char $;
  IF INPUT(age_char,best.) NE . OR age_char=' '
    THEN age=INPUT(age_char,BEST.);
    ELSE flag+1;
  IF INPUT(weight_char,BEST.) NE . OR weight_char=' '
    THEN weight=INPUT(weight_char,BEST.);
    ELSE flag+2;
  IF INPUT(height_char,best.) NE . OR height_char=' '
    THEN height=INPUT(height_char,BEST.);
    ELSE flag+4;

  IF flag=0
    THEN OUTPUT work.charin;
    ELSE OUTPUT work.errors;
RUN;
```

5.4.5 Converting Data between z/OS and Other Platforms

Converting data from z/OS systems to make it compatible with systems on other platforms is a big topic. It could be described in part as "The EBCDIC character set is not the same as ASCII," but there are also major differences in the way z/OS stores numeric data compared to the other systems. Fortunately, SAS software incorporates a large range of character and numeric informats that help to circumvent these differences. However, before I talk about these informats, there are two special situations where the differences are catered for automatically.

Where SAS software is installed on both platforms, all the conversion work can be done automatically by SAS, if the extract is read into SAS data sets on the z/OS system and transferred to the other system as SAS data. If SAS/CONNECT is not used to connect the two platforms, PROC CPORT can be used to create a platform-independent transfer file, and then PROC CIMPORT can be used to re-create the SAS data set from the transferred file. SAS/CONNECT actually uses the facilities provided by PROC CPORT and PROC CIMPORT to translate the character data in the SAS data set from EBCDIC to ASCII while it is transferring the data.

Example 5.1 Using PROC CPORT and PROC CIMPORT

On z/OS:

```
FILENAME cport 'transfer.trn' LRECL=80 RECFM=FB BLKSIZE=8000;

DATA transfer;
  * EBCDIC data file *;
  INFILE 'zos.dat' TRUNCOVER LRECL=33 RECFM=FB BLKSIZE=9900;
  INFORMAT name $8. sex $1. age weight height 8.;
  INPUT @1 name $ @9 sex $ @10 age @18 weight @26 height;
RUN;

PROC CPORT DATA=transfer FILE=cport;
RUN;
```

On Windows, after the transfer from z/OS, using FTP with the BINARY option:

```
FILENAME cport 'transfer.trn';

PROC CIMPORT INFILE=cport DATA=received;
RUN;
```

Example 5.2 Using SAS/CONNECT

On Windows:

```
RSUBMIT;
  DATA transfer;
    * EBCDIC data file *;
    INFILE 'zos.dat' TRUNCOVER LRECL=33 RECFM=FB BLKSIZE=9900;
    INFORMAT name $8. sex $1. age weight height 8.;
    INPUT @1 name $ @9 sex $ @10 age @18 weight @26 height;
  RUN;

  PROC DOWNLOAD DATA=transfer OUT=received;
  RUN;
ENDRSUBMIT;
```

The next two examples apply to transfers where SAS software is installed only on the receiving platforms, and the extract file contains only textual data— i.e, character fields and numeric data as text. Then the transfer of the extract file can be carried out using the ASCII option, so that all the data characters are converted from EBCDIC to ASCII. Note that any numeric data stored in binary or packed data formats will be corrupted by this method.

Example 5.3 Character-Based Data

On Windows, after the transfer of the file from z/OS, using FTP with the ASCII option:

```
DATA received;
  * ASCII text file *;
  INFILE 'transfer.dat' TRUNCOVER LRECL=33 RECFM=F;
  INFORMAT name $8. sex $1. age weight height 8.;
  INPUT @1 name $ @9 sex $ @10 age @18 weight @26 height;
RUN;
```

So what can you do if the extract data contains numeric data stored in binary or packed data formats? Now you can use the informats I mentioned earlier. After transferring the extract file using the BINARY option, the data itself is in z/OS format, so the character data is still in EBCDIC and the numeric data is in z/OS native format. In Example 3, the character items are read using the $EBCDIC informat and the textual numeric items are read using the S370FF informat.

Example 5.4 Unconverted Data

On Windows, after the transfer of the file from z/OS, using FTP with the BINARY option:

```
DATA received;
  * EBCDIC data file *;
  INFILE 'zos.dat' TRUNCOVER LRECL=33 RECFM=F;
  INFORMAT name $EBCDIC8. sex $EBCDIC1.
           age weight height S370FF8.;
  INPUT @1 name $ @9 sex $ @10 age @18 weight @26 height;
RUN;
```

Table 5.1 Numeric Informats That Can Be Used to Read z/OS Data (and Their Standard Equivalents)

SAS Numeric Informat	Function
S370FFw.d (w.d)	used on other computer systems to read EBCDIC data
S370FHEXw.d (HEXw.d)	reads real binary (floating-point) values in EBCDIC hexadecimal representation (new in SAS 8.2)
S370FIBw.d (IBw.d)	reads integer binary data
S370FIBUw.d	reads unsigned integer binary data
S370FPDw.d (PDw.d)	reads packed decimal data
S370FPDUw.d	reads unsigned packed decimal data
S370FPIBw.d (PIBw.d)	reads positive integer binary data
S370FRBw.d (RBw.d)	reads real binary data
S370FZDw.d (ZDw.d)	reads zoned decimal data
S370FZDLw.d	reads zoned decimal leading sign data
S370FZDSw.d	reads zoned decimal separate leading sign data
S370FZDTw.d	reads zoned decimal separate trailing sign data
S370FZDUw.d	reads unsigned zoned decimal data

5.4.6 Accessing Data in Spreadsheets

There are a number of methods for accessing spreadsheet data on the Windows platform without having to license SAS/ACCESS. Some methods rely on the spreadsheet software being installed on the same system, e.g., DDE (Dynamic Data Exchange) and OLE (Object Linking and Embedding). DDE has been well documented for accessing Excel spreadsheets. OLE can be used to access data in Excel and Lotus 1-2-3 spreadsheets. It is also possible to directly read the contents of the spreadsheet files, and then convert the internal data structure using SAS code, which can be employed to input data from StarOffice and OpenOffice.org spreadsheets. All these methods are described in the following sections.

5.4.7 DDE (Windows Only)

It should be noted that DDE is not a fast interface and is suitable only for transferring small amounts of data from spreadsheets into SAS data sets.

Exporting to Microsoft Excel

The following example sends data from a SAS session to an Excel spreadsheet. The target cells are rows 1 through 100 and columns 1 through 3. To do this, submit the following program:

```
/* The DDE link is established using   */
/* Microsoft Excel SHEET1, rows 1      */
/* through 100 and columns 1 through 3 */

FILENAME random DDE 'excel|sheet1!r1c1:r100c3';

DATA _NULL_;
  FILE random;
  DO i = 1 TO 100;
    x = RANUNI(i);
    y = 10 + x;
    z = x - 10;
    PUT x y z;
  END;
RUN;
```

Importing from Microsoft Excel

You can also use DDE to read data from an Excel application into SAS, as in the following example:

```
/* The DDE link is established using   */
/* Microsoft Excel SHEET1, rows 1      */
/* through 10 and columns 1 through 3  */

FILENAME monthly DDE 'excel|sheet1!r1c1:r10c3';

DATA mondata;
   INFILE monthly;
   INPUT var1 var2 var3;
RUN;
```

5.4.8 OLE (Windows Only)

This method requires code to be written in SCL, rather than Base SAS code. This will necessitate licensing only SAS/AF for the application developer, because Base SAS users can run SAS/AF applications without SAS/AF licenses. It should be noted that OLE is not a fast interface and is only suitable for transferring small amounts of data from spreadsheets into SAS data sets.

Exporting to Microsoft Excel

1. Load an instance of the OLE Automation class and invoke Excel. Set the object to Visible so you can see the automation in progress.

```
launchxl:
  hostcl = LOADCLASS('sashelp.fsp.hauto');
  CALL SEND(hostcl, '_NEW', excelobj, 0, 'Excel.Application');
  CALL SEND(excelobj, '_SETPROPERTY', 'Visible', 'True');
RETURN;
```

2. Get the identifier for the current Workbooks property and add a worksheet. Then get the identifier for the new worksheet.

```
createws:
  CALL SEND(excelobj, '_GETPROPERTY', 'Workbooks', wbsobj);
  CALL SEND(wbsobj, '_DO', 'Add' );
  CALL SEND(excelobj, '_GETPROPERTY', 'ActiveSheet', wsobj);
```

3. Open a SAS data set.

```
dsid = OPEN('sasuser.class', 'i');
CALL SET(dsid);
rc = FETCH(dsid);
nvar = ATTRN(dsid, 'NVARS');
nobs = ATTRN(dsid, 'NOBS');
```

4. Traverse the data set and populate the cells of the Excel worksheet with its data, row by row.

```
DO col = 1 TO nvar;
  CALL SEND(wsobj, '_COMPUTE', 'Cells', 1, col, retcell);
  var = VARNAME(dsid, col);
  CALL SEND(retcell, '_SETPROPERTY', 'Value', var);
END;
DO WHILE (rc NE -1);
  DO row = 1 TO nobs;
    DO col = 1 TO nvar;
      r = row + 1;
      CALL SEND(wsobj, '_COMPUTE', 'Cells', r, col, retcell);
      IF VARTYPE(dsid, col) EQ 'N'
        THEN var = GETVARN(dsid, col);
        ELSE var = GETVARC(dsid, col);
      CALL SEND(retcell, '_SETPROPERTY', 'Value', var);
    END;
    rc = FETCH(dsid);
  END;
```

```
      END;
      dsid = CLOSE(dsid);
   RETURN;
```

5. Close the worksheet and end the Excel session. The **_TERM** method deletes the OLE automation instance.

```
quitxl:
   CALL SEND(excelobj, '_GETPROPERTY', 'ActiveWorkbook', awbobj);
   CALL SEND(awbobj,  '_DO', 'Close', 'False');
   CALL SEND(excelobj, '_DO', 'Quit');
   CALL SEND(excelobj, '_TERM');
RETURN;
```

Importing from Microsoft Excel

The following code requires Excel to be installed on the same Windows system as that running the SAS code. An example of a typical Base SAS program to call this code is given:

```
%let dsn = sasuser.timesheet;
%let path = c:\temp;
%let file = timesheet.xls;
%let sheet = B;
%let from = A1;
%let to = T350;
dm 'af c=sasuser.excel.import.scl';
```

The following SCL code sets up the variables used in the application:

```
*------------------------------------------------------------*;
* Program : import.scl                                       *;
* Comments: Import SAS data set from Excel file.             *;
* Macvars : &file = Excel file to import                     *;
*           &path = path to file                             *;
*           &sheet = sheet to import                         *;
*           &from = starting cell to import                  *;
*           &to = finishing cell to import                   *;
*           &dsn = name of SAS data set                      *;
*------------------------------------------------------------*;
  LENGTH dsn $32
         sheetfile sheetpath sheet sheettextcol sheetname adname $80
          alpha alpha1 $27
          textcol $8 char1-char256 $80 fmt1-fmt256 $32;
  ARRAY char {*} char1-char256;
  ARRAY num {*} num1-num256;
  ARRAY fmt {*} fmt1-fmt256;
```

The **init** section is run automatically when the SCL application is started, and reads the parameters in from the SAS macro variables:

```
init:
  /* Initialize values */
  dsn = SYMGETC('dsn');
  tempdsn = 'work.excel';
  sheetfile = SYMGETC('file');
  sheetpath = SYMGETC('path');
  sheet = SYMGETC('sheet');
  fromcell = SYMGETC('from');
  tocell = SYMGETC('to');
  alpha = ' abcdefghijklmnopqrstuvwxyz';
  alpha1 = SUBSTR(alpha, 2);
  offset0 = INDEXC(fromcell, '0123456789');
  offset1 = INDEXC(tocell, '0123456789');
  IF offset0 = 2
    THEN sheetwidth0 = INDEX(alpha1,
                        LOWCASE(SUBSTR(fromcell, 1, 1)));
    ELSE sheetwidth0 = INDEX(alpha1,
                      LOWCASE(SUBSTR(fromcell, 1, 1))) * 26 +
                      INDEX(alpha1,
                        LOWCASE(SUBSTR(fromcell, 2, 2)));
  IF offset1 = 2
    THEN sheetwidth1 = INDEX(alpha1,
                        LOWCASE(SUBSTR(tocell, 1, 1)));
    ELSE sheetwidth1 = INDEX(alpha1,
                        LOWCASE(SUBSTR(tocell, 1, 1))) * 26 +
                      INDEX(alpha1,
                        LOWCASE(SUBSTR(tocell, 2, 2)));
  sheetdepth0 = INPUT(SUBSTR(fromcell, offset0), 8.);
  sheetdepth1 = INPUT(SUBSTR(tocell, offset1), 8.);
RETURN;
```

The **main** section is run after the **init** section, and controls the whole application by starting the code to launch Excel, open the existing Excel spreadsheet, copy the selected cells to the SAS data set, and finally close Excel:

```
main:
  LINK b_launch;
  LINK b_create;
  LINK b_exit;
RETURN;
```

The **term** section runs when the application is about to close, and is used to tidy up any resources that have been left behind from the other processing sections, e.g., closing open SAS data sets:

```
term:
  /* Close SAS data set, if open */
  IF dsid > 0 THEN dsid = CLOSE(dsid);
  rc = rc;
  fromcell = fromcell;
  tocell = tocell;
RETURN;
```

The **b_launch** section is called by the **main** section, and launches a new Excel application:

```
b_launch:
  /* Open Excel, and make visible */
  hostcl = LOADCLASS('sashelp.fsp.hauto');
  CALL SEND(hostcl, '_NEW', excelobj, 0, 'Excel.Application');
  CALL SEND(excelobj, '_SETPROPERTY', 'Visible', 'True');
RETURN;
```

The **b_create** section is called by the **main** section, opens the existing Excel spreadsheet, and copies the selected cells to the SAS data set:

```
b_create:
  /* Open existing document */
  CALL SEND(excelobj, '_GETPROPERTY', 'workbooks', adsobj);
  CALL SEND(adsobj, '_DO', 'Open',
            trim(sheetpath) !! '\' !! sheetfile, 0, 'True');
  CALL SEND(excelobj, '_GETPROPERTY', 'ActiveWorkbook', adobj);
  CALL SEND(adobj, '_GETPROPERTY', 'Name', adname);
  CALL SEND(adobj, '_GETPROPERTY', 'Worksheets', shsobj);
  CALL SEND(shsobj, '_GETPROPERTY', 'Count', sheetcount);
  put shsobj= sheetcount=;
  do i=1 to sheetcount;
    CALL SEND(adobj, '_COMPUTE', 'Worksheets', i, shobj);
    CALL SEND(shobj, '_GETPROPERTY', 'Name', sheetname);
    if upcase(sheetname) = upcase(sheet) then leave;
  end;
  /* Open SAS data set */
  dsid = OPEN(tempdsn, 'N');
  /* Create new columns */
  DO sheetcol = sheetwidth0 TO sheetwidth1;
  rc = NEWVAR(dsid, 'char' !! TRIM(LEFT(PUT(sheetcol, 8.))),
              'C', 80);
  rc = NEWVAR(dsid, 'fmt' !! TRIM(LEFT(PUT(sheetcol, 8.))),
              'C', 32);
  rc = NEWVAR(dsid, 'num' !! TRIM(LEFT(PUT(sheetcol, 8.))),
              'N');
  END;
```

```
IF dsid > 0 THEN dsid = CLOSE(dsid);
/* Write SAS data set row values using sheet cells */
dsid = OPEN(tempdsn, 'U');
CALL SET(dsid);
DO row = (sheetdepth0 - 1) TO (sheetdepth1 - 1);
  sheetrow = row + 1;
  rc = APPEND(dsid);
  DO col = (sheetwidth0 - 1) TO (sheetwidth1 - 1);
    sheetcol = col + 1;
    LINK col2text;
    sheettextcol = TRIM(textcol) !! ":" !! textcol;
    CALL SEND(shobj, '_COMPUTE', 'Range',
              textcol, textcol, ranobj);
    CALL SEND(shobj, '_DO', 'Activate');
    CALL SEND(ranobj, '_GETPROPERTY', 'NumberFormat',
              fmt[sheetcol]);
    CALL SEND(ranobj, '_GETPROPERTY', 'Text',
              char[sheetcol]);
  END;
  /* Omit blank rows from SAS data set */
  flag = 0;
  DO sheetcol = sheetwidth0 TO sheetwidth1;
    IF char[sheetcol] NE ' ' THEN flag + 1;
  END;
  IF flag > 0
    THEN rc = UPDATE(dsid);
    ELSE rc = DELOBS(dsid);
END;
IF dsid > 0 THEN dsid = CLOSE(dsid);
SUBMIT;
  PROC TRANSPOSE DATA = work.excel (KEEP = fmt:)
                 OUT = work.transposexlsa
                 NAME = fmt;
    VAR fmt:;
  RUN;
  PROC SORT DATA = work.transposexlsa;
    BY fmt;
  RUN;
  PROC TRANSPOSE DATA = work.transposexlsa
                 OUT = work.transposexlsb
                 NAME = col;
    BY fmt;
    VAR col:;
  RUN;
```

```
PROC FREQ DATA = work.transposexlsb NOPRINT;
  BY fmt;
  TABLES col1 / OUT = work.countxls;
RUN;
PROC SORT DATA = work.countxls;
  BY fmt DESCENDING count;
RUN;
FILENAME __temp CATALOG 'work.excel';
DATA _NULL_;
  SET work.countxls;
  BY fmt;
  FILE __temp(format.source);
  IF _N_ = 1 THEN PUT 'format';
  IF first.fmt THEN DO;
    SELECT;
      WHEN (col1 = :'£')
        PUT @2 fmt ' NLMNLGBP.' @2 'num';
      WHEN (col1 = :'$')
        PUT @2 fmt ' NLMNLUSD.' @2 'num';
      WHEN (index(col1, '-mmm') > 0)
        PUT @2 fmt ' DATE.' @2 'num';
      WHEN (index(col1, ':mm') > 0)
        PUT @2 fmt ' TIME.' @2 'num';
      OTHERWISE;
    END;
  END;
RUN;
DATA &dsn (DROP = fmt: i);
  SET work.excel;
  ARRAY fmt {*} fmt:;
  ARRAY char {*} char:;
  ARRAY num {*} num:;
  DO i = 1 TO DIM(fmt);
    SELECT;
      WHEN (fmt[i] = :'£')
        num[i] = INPUT(SUBSTR(LEFT(char[i]), 2), COMMA20.);
      WHEN (fmt[i] = :'$')
        num[i] = INPUT(SUBSTR(LEFT(char[i]), 2), COMMA20.);
      WHEN (index(fmt[i], '-mmm') > 0)
        num[i] = INPUT(LEFT(char[i]), DATE12.);
      WHEN (index(fmt[i], ':mm') > 0)
        num[i] = INPUT(LEFT(char[i]), TIME12.);
      OTHERWISE DO;
        num[i] = INPUT(LEFT(char[i]), ? 20.);
        IF num[i] = .   THEN
          num[i] = INPUT(LEFT(char[i]), ? COMMA20.);
      END;
```

```
        END;
      END;
      %INCLUDE __temp(format.source) / SOURCE2;;
    RUN;
    FILENAME __temp CLEAR;
  ENDSUBMIT;
RETURN;
```

The **b_exit** section is called by the **main** section, and closes the Excel application:

```
b_exit:
  /* Close Excel and application */
  CALL SEND(excelobj, '_DO', 'Quit');
  CALL SEND(excelobj, '_TERM');
  CALL EXECCMD('CANCEL;');
RETURN;
```

The **col2text** section is called by the **b_create** section, and converts the SAS data set column and row to Excel cell notation:

```
col2text:
  /* Convert SAS data set column and row
     to Excel cell notation: e.g. "4,25" to "d25" */
  IF sheetcol < 27
  THEN textcol = LEFT(SUBSTR(alpha, INT(sheetcol/27) + 1, 1) !!
                      SUBSTR(alpha1, MOD(col, 26) + 1, 1) !!
                      TRIM(LEFT(PUT(sheetrow, 8.)))
                     );
    ELSE textcol = LEFT(SUBSTR(alpha1, INT(col/26) + 1, 1) !!
                        SUBSTR(alpha1, MOD(col, 26) + 1, 1) !!
                        TRIM(LEFT(PUT(sheetrow, 8.)))
                       );
  RETURN;
```

Exporting to Lotus 1-2-3

The following code requires Lotus 1-2-3 Version 9 to be installed on the same Windows system as that running the SAS code. An example of a typical Base SAS program to call this code is given:

```
%let dsn = sashelp.prdsale;
%let rows = 50;
%let sheet = c:\temp\test.123;
dm 'af c=sasuser.lotus123.export.scl';
```

The following SCL code sets up the variables used in the application:

```
*-------------------------------------------------------------*;
* Program : export.scl                                        *;
* Comments: Export SAS data set into Lotus 123 file.          *;
* Macvars : &dsn = name of SAS data set to export             *;
*           &rows = maximum number of rows to export          *;
*           &sheet = Lotus 123 file                           *;
*-------------------------------------------------------------*;
  LENGTH dsn $17 sheetfile $80 alpha $27 textcol $8 varf $16;
```

The **init** section is run automatically when the SCL application is started, and reads the parameters in from the SAS macro variables:

```
init:
  /* Initialize values */
  dsn = SCAN(SYMGETC('dsn'), 1, '(,)'); *ignore data set
options*;
  sheetfile = SYMGETC('sheet');
  maxrows = SYMGETN('rows');
  alpha = ' abcdefghijklmnopqrstuvwxyz';
RETURN;
```

The **main** section is run after the **init** section, and controls the whole application by starting the code to launch 1-2-3, create a new 1-2-3 spreadsheet, copy the selected rows from the SAS data set, close the worksheet, and finally close 1-2-3:

```
main:
  LINK b_launch;
  LINK b_create;
  LINK b_close;
  LINK b_exit;
RETURN;
```

The **term** section runs when the application is about to close, and is used to tidy up any resources that have been left behind from the other processing sections, e.g., closing open SAS data sets:

```
term:
  /* Close SAS data set, if open */
  IF dsid > 0 THEN dsid = CLOSE(dsid);
RETURN;
```

The **b_launch** section is called by the **main** section, and creates a new 1-2-3 spreadsheet:

```
b_launch:
  /* Open 1-2-3, and make visible */
  hostcl = LOADCLASS('sashelp.fsp.hauto');
  CALL SEND(hostcl, '_NEW', sessobj, 0, 'Lotus123.Workbook.98');
  CALL SEND(sessobj, '_GETPROPERTY', 'Application', appobj);
  CALL SEND(appobj, '_SETPROPERTY', 'Visible', 'True');
RETURN;
```

The **b_create** section is called by the **main** section, and copies the selected rows from the SAS data set:

```
b_create:
  /* Create new document */
  CALL SEND(appobj, '_DO', 'NewDocument');
  CALL SEND(appobj, '_GETPROPERTY', 'ActiveDocument', adobj);
  /* Open SAS data set, and count columns and rows */
  dsid = OPEN(dsn, 'I');
  CALL SET(dsid);
  rc = FETCH(dsid);
  nvar = ATTRN(dsid, 'NVARS');
  nobs = ATTRN(dsid, 'NOBS');
  IF nobs = . OR nobs > maxrows THEN nobs = maxrows;
  /* Write column names to 1st row of sheet */
  DO col = 0 TO (nvar - 1);
    sheetcol = col + 1;
    sheetrow = 1;
    LINK col2text;
    CALL SEND(adobj, '_GETPROPERTY', 'Ranges',
              TRIM(textcol), retcell);
    var = VARNAME(dsid, sheetcol);
    CALL SEND(retcell, '_SETPROPERTY', 'Contents', var);
  END;
  /* Write SAS data set row values to sheet rows */
  DO row = 0 TO (nobs - 1);
    sheetrow = row + 2;
    DO col = 0 TO (nvar - 1);
      sheetcol = col + 1;
      LINK col2text;
      CALL SEND(adobj, '_GETPROPERTY', 'Ranges',
                TRIM(textcol), retcell);
      varf = VARFMT(dsid, sheetcol);
      IF VARTYPE(dsid, sheetcol) EQ 'N'
        THEN var = PUTN(GETVARN(dsid, sheetcol), varf);
        ELSE var = PUTC(GETVARC(dsid, sheetcol), varf);
      CALL SEND(retcell, '_SETPROPERTY', 'Contents', var);
    END;
```

```
      rc = FETCH(dsid);
      IF rc = -1 THEN LEAVE;
    END;
  RETURN;
```

The **b_close** section is called by the **main** section, and saves and closes the 1-2-3 worksheet:

```
b_close:
  /* Save and close sheet */
  CALL SEND(adobj, '_DO', 'SaveAs', sheetfile);
  CALL SEND(appobj, '_GETPROPERTY', 'ApplicationWindow', awobj);
  CALL SEND(awobj, '_DO', 'Close', 'False');
RETURN;
```

The **b_exit** section is called by the **main** section, and closes the 1-2-3 application:

```
b_exit:
  /* Close 1-2-3 and application */
  CALL SEND(appobj, '_DO', 'Quit');
  CALL SEND(appobj, '_TERM');
  CALL EXECCMD('CANCEL;');
RETURN;
```

The **col2text** section is called by the **b_create** section, and converts the SAS data set column and row to 1-2-3 cell notation:

```
col2text:
  /* Convert SAS data set column and row
     to 1-2-3 cell notation: e.g. "4,25" to "d25" */
  textcol = LEFT(SUBSTR(alpha, INT(sheetcol / 27) + 1, 1) !!
               SUBSTR(alpha, MOD(sheetcol, 27) + 1, 1) !!
               TRIM(LEFT(PUT(sheetrow, 8.)))
             );
RETURN;
```

Importing from Lotus 1-2-3

The following code requires Lotus 1-2-3 Version 9 to be installed on the same Windows system as that running the SAS code. An example of a typical Base SAS program to call this code is given:

```
%let dsn = sasuser.timesheet;
%let path = c:\temp;
%let file = timesheet.123;
%let sheet = B;
```

```
%let from = A1;
%let to = T350;
dm 'af c=sasuser.lotus123.import.scl';
```

The following SCL code sets up the variables used in the application:

```
*-------------------------------------------------------------*;
* Program : import.scl                                        *;
* Comments: Import SAS data set from Lotus 123 file.          *;
* Macvars : &file = Lotus 123 file to import                  *;
*           &path = path to file                              *;
*           &sheet = sheet to import                          *;
*           &from = starting cell to import                   *;
*           &to = finishing cell to import                    *;
*           &dsn = name of SAS data set                       *;
*-------------------------------------------------------------*;
LENGTH dsn $32
       sheetfile sheetpath sheet sheettextcol sheetname adname
$80
       alpha alpha1 $27
       textcol $8 char1-char256 $80 fmt1-fmt256 $32;
ARRAY char {*} char1-char256;
ARRAY num {*} num1-num256;
ARRAY fmt {*} fmt1-fmt256;
```

The **init** section is run automatically when the SCL application is started, and reads the parameters in from the SAS macro variables:

```
init:
  /* Initialize values */
  dsn = SYMGETC('dsn');
  tempdsn = 'work.lotus123';
  sheetfile = SYMGETC('file');
  sheetpath = SYMGETC('path');
  sheet = SYMGETC('sheet');
  fromcell = SYMGETC('from');
  tocell = SYMGETC('to');
  alpha = ' abcdefghijklmnopqrstuvwxyz';
  alpha1 = SUBSTR(alpha, 2);
  offset0 = INDEXC(fromcell, '0123456789');
  offset1 = INDEXC(tocell, '0123456789');
  IF offset0 = 2
    THEN sheetwidth0 = INDEX(alpha1,
                       LOWCASE(SUBSTR(fromcell, 1, 1)));
    ELSE sheetwidth0 = INDEX(alpha1,
                       LOWCASE(SUBSTR(fromcell, 1, 1))) * 26+
                       INDEX(alpha1,
                       LOWCASE(SUBSTR(fromcell, 2, 2)));
  IF offset1 = 2
```

```
      THEN sheetwidth1 = INDEX(alpha1,
                              LOWCASE(SUBSTR(tocell, 1, 1)));
      ELSE sheetwidth1 = INDEX(alpha1,
                              LOWCASE(SUBSTR(tocell, 1, 1))) * 26 +
                         INDEX(alpha1,
                              LOWCASE(SUBSTR(tocell, 2, 2)));
   sheetdepth0 = INPUT(SUBSTR(fromcell, offset0), 8.);
   sheetdepth1 = INPUT(SUBSTR(tocell, offset1), 8.);
RETURN;
```

The **main** section is run after the **init** section, and controls the whole application by starting the code to launch 1-2-3, open the existing 1-2-3 spreadsheet, and copy the selected cells to the SAS data set, close the worksheet, and finally close 1-2-3:

```
main:
   LINK b_launch;
   LINK b_create;
   LINK b_close;
   LINK b_exit;
RETURN;
```

The **term** section runs when the application is about to close, and is used to tidy up any resources that have been left behind from the other processing sections, e.g., closing open SAS data sets:

```
term:
   /* Close SAS data set, if open */
   IF dsid > 0 THEN dsid = CLOSE(dsid);
   rc = rc;
   fromcell = fromcell;
   tocell = tocell;
RETURN;
```

The **b_launch** section is called by the **main** section, and launches a new 1-2-3 application:

```
b_launch:
   /* Open 1-2-3, and make visible */
   hostcl = LOADCLASS('sashelp.fsp.hauto');
   CALL SEND(hostcl, '_NEW', sessobj, 0, 'Lotus123.Workbook.98');
   CALL SEND(sessobj, '_GETPROPERTY', 'Application', appobj);
   CALL SEND(appobj, '_SETPROPERTY', 'Visible', 'True');
RETURN;
```

The **b_create** section is called by the **main** section, opens the existing 1-2-3 spreadsheet, and copies the selected cells to the SAS data set:

```
b_create:
  /* Open existing document */
  CALL SEND(appobj, '_DO', 'OPENDOCUMENT', sheetfile, sheetpath);
  CALL SEND(appobj, '_GETPROPERTY', 'Documents', adsobj);
  CALL SEND(adsobj, '_GETPROPERTY', 'Count', doccount);
  CALL SEND(appobj, '_GETPROPERTY', 'ActiveDocument', adobj);
  CALL SEND(adobj, '_GETPROPERTY', 'Name', adname);
  IF doccount GE 2 THEN DO i = 2 TO doccount;
    IF INDEX(UPCASE(TRIM(REVERSE(adname))),
             UPCASE(TRIM(REVERSE(sheetfile)))) = 1
      THEN DO;
        CALL SEND(adsobj, '_GETPROPERTY', 'Next', adobj);
        CALL SEND(adobj, '_GETPROPERTY', 'Name', adname);
      END;
      ELSE LEAVE;
  END;
  CALL SEND(adobj, '_GETPROPERTY', 'Sheets', shsobj);
  CALL SEND(shsobj, '_GETPROPERTY', 'Count', sheetcount);
  CALL SEND(adobj, '_GETPROPERTY', 'CurrentSheet', shobj);
  CALL SEND(shobj, '_GETPROPERTY', 'Name', sheetname);
  IF sheetcount GE 2 THEN DO i = 2 TO sheetcount;
    IF UPCASE(sheetname) NE UPCASE(sheet)
      THEN DO;
        CALL SEND(shsobj, '_COMPUTE', 'Next', shobj);
        CALL SEND(shobj, '_GETPROPERTY', 'Name', sheetname);
      END;
      ELSE LEAVE;
  END;
  CALL SEND(shobj, '_DO', 'TurnTo');
  /* Open SAS data set */
  dsid = OPEN(tempdsn, 'N');
  /* Create new columns */
  DO sheetcol = sheetwidth0 TO sheetwidth1;
    rc = NEWVAR(dsid, 'char' !! TRIM(LEFT(PUT(sheetcol, 8.))),
                'C', 80);
    rc = NEWVAR(dsid, 'fmt' !! TRIM(LEFT(PUT(sheetcol, 8.))),
                'C', 32);
    rc = NEWVAR(dsid, 'num' !! TRIM(LEFT(PUT(sheetcol, 8.))),
                'N');
  END;
  IF dsid > 0 THEN dsid = CLOSE(dsid);
  /* Write SAS data set row values using sheet cells */
  dsid = OPEN(tempdsn, 'U');
  CALL SET(dsid);
```

```
      DO row = (sheetdepth0 - 1) TO (sheetdepth1 - 1);
        sheetrow = row + 1;
        rc = APPEND(dsid);
        DO col = (sheetwidth0 - 1) TO (sheetwidth1 - 1);
          sheetcol = col + 1;
          LINK col2text;
          sheettextcol = TRIM(sheet) !! ":" !! textcol;
          CALL SEND(adobj, '_GETPROPERTY', 'Ranges',
                    TRIM(sheettextcol), ranobj);
          CALL SEND(ranobj, '_GETPROPERTY', 'FormatName',
                    fmt[sheetcol]);
          CALL SEND(ranobj, '_GETPROPERTY', 'CellDisplay',
                    char[sheetcol]);
        END;
        /* Omit blank rows from SAS data set */
        flag = 0;
        DO sheetcol = sheetwidth0 TO sheetwidth1;
          IF char[sheetcol] NE ' ' THEN flag + 1;
        END;
        IF flag > 0
          THEN rc = UPDATE(dsid);
          ELSE rc = DELOBS(dsid);
      end;
      IF dsid > 0 THEN dsid = CLOSE(dsid);

      SUBMIT;

        PROC TRANSPOSE DATA = work.lotus123 (KEEP = fmt:)
                       OUT = work.transpose123a
                       NAME = fmt;
          VAR fmt:;
        RUN;

        PROC SORT DATA = work.transpose123a;
          BY fmt;
        RUN;

        PROC TRANSPOSE DATA = work.transpose123a
                       OUT = work.transpose123b
                       NAME = col;
          BY fmt;
          VAR col:;
        RUN;
```

```
PROC FREQ DATA = work.transpose123b NOPRINT;
  BY fmt;
  TABLES col1 / OUT = work.count123;
RUN;

PROC SORT DATA = work.count123;
  BY fmt DESCENDING count;
RUN;

FILENAME __temp CATALOG 'work.lotus123';
DATA _NULL_;
  SET work.count123;
  BY fmt;
  FILE __temp(format.source);
  IF _N_ = 1 THEN PUT 'format';
  IF first.fmt THEN DO;
    SELECT (col1);
      WHEN ('British Pound')
        PUT @2 fmt ' NLMNLGBP.' @2 'num';
      WHEN ('31-Dec-96')
        PUT @2 fmt ' DATE.' @2 'num';
      WHEN ('Time Short International')
        PUT @2 fmt ' TIME.' @2 'num';
      OTHERWISE;
    END;
  END;
RUN;
DATA &dsn (DROP = fmt: i);
  SET work.lotus123;
  ARRAY fmt {*} fmt:;
  ARRAY char {*} char:;
  ARRAY num {*} num:;
  DO i = 1 TO DIM(fmt);
    SELECT (fmt[i]);
      WHEN ('British Pound')
        num[i] = INPUT(SUBSTR(LEFT(char[i]), 2), COMMA20.);
      WHEN ('31-Dec-96')
        num[i] = INPUT(LEFT(char[i]), DATE12.);
      WHEN ('Time Short International')
        num[i] = INPUT(LEFT(char[i]), TIME12.);
      OTHERWISE DO;
        num[i] = INPUT(LEFT(char[i]), ? 20.);
        IF num[i] = .  THEN
          num[i] = INPUT(LEFT(char[i]), ? COMMA20.);
      END;
    END;
  END;
```

```
      %INCLUDE __temp(format.source) / SOURCE2;
      ;
   RUN;

   FILENAME __temp CLEAR;

 ENDSUBMIT;
RETURN;
```

The **b_close** section is called by the **main** section, and closes the 1-2-3 worksheet:

```
b_close:
  /* Close sheet */
  CALL SEND(appobj, '_GETPROPERTY', 'ApplicationWindow', awobj);
  CALL SEND(awobj, '_DO', 'Close', 'False');
RETURN;
```

The **b_exit** section is called by the **main** section, and closes the 1-2-3 application:

```
b_exit:
  /* Close 1-2-3 and application */
  CALL SEND(appobj, '_DO', 'Quit');
  CALL SEND(appobj, '_TERM');
  CALL EXECCMD('CANCEL;');
RETURN;
```

The **col2text** section is called by the **b_create** section, and converts the SAS data set column and row to 1-2-3 cell notation:

```
col2text:
  /* Convert SAS data set column and row
     to 1-2-3 cell notation: e.g. "4,25" to "d25" */
  IF sheetcol < 27
    THEN textcol = LEFT(SUBSTR(alpha, INT(sheetcol/27) + 1, 1) !!
                        SUBSTR(alpha1, MOD(col, 26) + 1, 1) !!
                        TRIM(LEFT(PUT(sheetrow, 8.)))
                       );
    ELSE textcol = LEFT(SUBSTR(alpha1, INT(col/26) + 1, 1) !!
                        SUBSTR(alpha1, MOD(col, 26) + 1, 1) !!
                        TRIM(LEFT(PUT(sheetrow, 8.)))
                       );
RETURN;
```

5.4.9 Reading Spreadsheet Files as Raw Data (Windows, Linux, and UNIX)

StarOffice and OpenOffice.org

Data in StarOffice and OpenOffice.org is stored as XML in a zipped file. The detailed spreadsheet data is contained in the **content.xml** file inside the zipped file—i.e., ***.sxc** (StarOffice XML spreadsheet) for Version 1.1 or ***.ods** (OpenDocument spreadsheet) for Version 2.0+, which can be simply processed using DATA step SAS code to create a number of SAS data sets of character variables (i.e., VAR1, VAR2, etc.), one for each worksheet. The character variables can then be converted, as appropriate, to numeric values. The following program assumes that the **content.xml** file has already been unzipped from the ***.sxc** or ***.ods** file into a folder referenced by a FILENAME statement, e.g.:

```
        FILENAME _sxcdir '~/tmp';  * in Linux or UNIX *;
```
or
```
        FILENAME _sxcdir 'c:\temp';  * in Windows *;
```

This step processes the **content.xml** file into a new XML file called **temp1.xml** to make certain all the XML tags are on separate lines, to make it easier to read into SAS.

```
        DATA _NULL_;
          INFILE __sxcdir(content.xml) RECFM = N LRECL = 32760 END =
      eof;
          FILE __sxcdir(temp1.xml) LRECL = 5120;
          LENGTH char1 $1;
          DO UNTIL (eof);
            INPUT char1 $CHAR1.;
            IF char1 = '>' THEN DO;
              PUT char1;
            END;
            ELSE IF char1 = '<' THEN DO;
              PUT;
              PUT char1 +(-1) @;
            END;
            ELSE PUT char1 +(-1) @;
          END;
          STOP;
        RUN;
```

Specific lines of the **temp1.xml** file are read into SAS and labeled according to their XML hierarchy.

```
DATA _xml (KEEP = _record _level _first _last _text);
  INFILE __sxcdir(temp1.xml) LRECL = 5120 TRUNCOVER;
  LENGTH _record _level _first _last 8 _text $1000;
  RETAIN _level 0;
  INPUT _text $CHAR1000.;
  _record = _N_;
  SELECT;
    WHEN (_text = :'<?xml')
      DO; _level = 0; _first = 1; END;
    WHEN (_text = :'<office:body ')
      DO; _level = 1; _first = 1; END;
    WHEN (_text = :'</office:body')
      DO; _level = 1; _last = 1; END;
    WHEN (_text = :'<table:table ')
      DO; _level = 2; _first = 1; END;
    WHEN (_text = :'</table:table>')
      DO; _level = 2; _last = 1; END;
    WHEN (_text = :'<table:table-row ')
      DO; _level = 3; _first = 1; END;
    WHEN (_text = :'</table:table-row')
      DO; _level = 3; _last = 1; END;
    WHEN (_text = :'<table:table-cell ')
      DO; _level = 4; _first = 1; END;
    WHEN (_text = :'</table:table-cell')
      DO; _level = 4; _last = 1; END;
    WHEN (_text = :'<office:') RETURN;
    WHEN (_text = :'</office:') RETURN;
    WHEN (_text = :'<style') RETURN;
    WHEN (_text = :'</style') RETURN;
    WHEN (_text = :'<number') RETURN;
    WHEN (_text = :'</number') RETURN;
    WHEN (_text = :'<table:') RETURN;
    WHEN (_text = :'</table:') RETURN;
    WHEN (_text = :'<text') RETURN;
    WHEN (_text = :'</text') RETURN;
    WHEN (_text = ' ') RETURN;
    OTHERWISE;
  END;
  IF _text = :'<?xml' OR _level > 0 THEN OUTPUT;
RUN;
```

XML tags specific to the worksheet are selected, and the range of XML records associated with each table are recorded. This information is used later to generate a SAS format that can be used to identify a worksheet from the record number of the original XML data.

```
DATA _xmltable (KEEP = _record_first _record_last _table);
  SET _xml;
  WHERE _level = 2;
  LENGTH _table $32;
  RETAIN _record_first _record_last . _table ' ';
  IF _first = 1 THEN DO;
    _table = TRANSLATE(TRIM(SCAN(_text, 2, '"')), '_', ' ');
    _record_first = _record;
    _record_last = .;
  END;
  ELSE IF _last = 1 THEN DO;
    _record_last = _record;
    OUTPUT;
  END;
RUN;


PROC SORT DATA = _xmltable;
  BY _table;
RUN;
```

The SAS format **rngtab** is now created from the **_xmltable** SAS data set:

```
DATA __cntlin (KEEP = fmtname start end label hlo type);
  LENGTH fmtname $7 start end label $32 hlo type $1;
  SET _xmltable;
  BY _table;
  hlo = ' ';
  fmtname = 'rngtab';
  type = 'N';
  start = TRIM(LEFT(PUT(_record_first, 16.)));
  end = TRIM(LEFT(PUT(_record_last, 16.)));
  label = _table;
  OUTPUT;
RUN;


PROC SORT DATA = __cntlin NODUPKEYS;
  BY fmtname start;
RUN;


PROC FORMAT CNTLIN = __cntlin;
RUN;
```

The occupied columns in each worksheet are counted, so that the SAS data sets can be created with the minimum number of columns:

```
DATA _xmlcolumn (KEEP = _table _columns);
  SET _xml;
  WHERE (_level IN (2, 4) AND _first = 1) OR _level = 3;
  LENGTH _table $32 _columns 8;
  RETAIN _table ' ' _columns .;
  IF _level = 2 THEN DO;
    _table = TRANSLATE(TRIM(SCAN(_text, 2, '"')), '_', ' ');
    RETURN;
  END;
  ELSE IF _level = 3 AND _first = 1 THEN DO;
    _columns = 0;
    RETURN;
  END;
  ELSE IF _level = 4 THEN DO;
    _columns + 1;
    RETURN;
  END;
  ELSE IF _level = 3 AND _last = 1 THEN DO;
    OUTPUT;
  END;
RUN;

PROC SUMMARY DATA = _xmlcolumn NWAY;
  CLASS _table;
  VAR _columns;
  OUTPUT OUT = _xmlcolumn2 (DROP = _freq_ _type_) MAX =;
RUN;

PROC SORT DATA = _xmlcolumn2;
  BY _table;
RUN;
```

The code fragments to create the individual SAS data sets in the WORK library and to write the XML data into the tables are generated as four catalog entries: **_data.source** (DATA and SET statements), **_process.source** (data processing code), **_output.source** (OUTPUT statements), and **_run.source** (closing and RUN statements). There is data-specific processing included for floating-point numeric, date, time, and currency data. These code fragments are run in sequence once the column data processing has been completed.

```
FILENAME __src CATALOG 'work._xml';

DATA _NULL_;
  SET _xmlcolumn2;
  IF _N_ = 1 THEN DO;
    FILE __src(_data.source);
    PUT 'DATA';
    FILE __src(_process.source);
    PUT '        ;';
    PUT '  SET _xml;';
    PUT '  WHERE _level IN (3, 4);';
    PUT '  LENGTH var1-var256 $1000 _type $16 _temp $1000;';
    PUT '  ARRAY v {*} var1-var256;';
    PUT '  RETAIN var1-var256 " " _count . _repeat . _type '  ';';
    PUT '  IF _level = 3 AND _first = 1 THEN DO;';
    PUT '    _count = 0;';
    PUT '    _repeat = .;';
    PUT '    DO _i = 1 TO DIM(v);';
    PUT '      v[_i]="";';
    PUT '    END;';
    PUT '  END;';
    PUT '  ELSE IF _level = 4 AND _first = 1 THEN DO;';
    PUT '    IF _repeat > 1 THEN DO _i = 1 TO (_repeat - 1);';
    PUT '      _count + 1;';
    PUT '      v[_count] = v[_count - 1];';
    PUT '    END;';
    PUT '    _type = "";';
    PUT '    _count + 1;';
    PUT '    _offset = INDEX(_text,';
    PUT '                    "table:number-columns-repeated=");';
    PUT '    IF _offset > 0 THEN
            _repeat = INPUT(SCAN(SUBSTR(_text, _offset +
                LENGTH("table:number-columns-repeated=") +
1),
                    1, """"), BEST.);';
    PUT '    ELSE _repeat = .;';
```

OpenOffice.org Version 1.1:

```
PUT '    _offset = INDEX(_text, "table:value-type=");';
```

OpenOffice.org Version 2.0+:

```
PUT '    _offset = INDEX(_text, "office:value-type=");';

PUT '    IF _offset > 0 THEN DO;';
```

OpenOffice.org Version 1.1:

```
PUT '          _type = SCAN(SUBSTR(_text, _offset +
                          LENGTH("table:value-type=") + 1),
```

OpenOffice.org Version 2.0+:

```
PUT '          _type = SCAN(SUBSTR(_text, _offset +
                          LENGTH("office:value-type=") + 1),

                          1, """");';
PUT '        SELECT (_type);';
PUT '          WHEN ("time") DO;';
```

OpenOffice.org Version 1.1:

```
PUT '            _offset = INDEX(_text, "table:time-value=");';
PUT '            _temp = SCAN(SUBSTR(_text,_offset +
                          LENGTH("table:time-value=") + 1),
```

OpenOffice.org Version 2.0+:

```
PUT '            _offset = INDEX(_text, "office:time-value=");';
PUT '            _temp = SCAN(SUBSTR(_text,_offset +
                          LENGTH("office:time-value=") + 1),

                          1, """");';
PUT '            v[_count] = PUT(hms(INPUT(SCAN(_temp, 1,
                                  "PTHMS"), BEST.),';
PUT '                              INPUT(SCAN(_temp, 2,
                                  "PTHMS"), BEST.),';
PUT '                              INPUT(TRANSLATE(
                                  SCAN(_temp, 3,
                                  "PTHMS"), ".", ","),
                                  BEST.)), TIME11.2);';
PUT '          END;';
PUT '          WHEN ("date") DO;';
```

OpenOffice.org Version 1.1:

```
PUT '            _offset = INDEX(_text, "table:date-value=");';
PUT '            _temp = SCAN(SUBSTR(_text, _offset +
                          LENGTH("table:date-value=") + 1),
```

OpenOffice.org Version 2.0+:

```
PUT '            _offset = INDEX(_text, "office:time-value=");';
PUT '            _temp = SCAN(SUBSTR(_text, _offset +
```

```
                                LENGTH("office:date-value=") + 1),

                         1, """");';
PUT '            if SCAN(_temp, 2, "T") NE " " then';
PUT '               v[_count] = PUT(DHMS(INPUT(SCAN(_temp, 1, "T"),
                                      YYMMDD10.),';
PUT '                             0, 0, INPUT(TRANSLATE(
                                      SCAN(_temp, 2, "T"),
                                      ".", ","), TIME11.)),
                                      DATETIME21.2);';
PUT '            ELSE';
PUT '               v[_count] = PUT(INPUT(SCAN(_temp, 1, "T"),
                                   YYMMDD10.), DATE9.);';
PUT '            END;';
PUT '         WHEN ("currency") DO;';
```

OpenOffice.org Version 1.1:

```
PUT '            _offset = INDEX(_text, "table:currency=");';
PUT '            v[_count] = SCAN(SUBSTR(_text, _offset +
                              LENGTH("table:currency=") + 1),
                              1, """");';
PUT '            _offset = INDEX(_text, "table:value=");';
PUT '            v[_count] = TRIM(v[_count]) !!
                           SCAN(SUBSTR(_text, _offset +
                           LENGTH("table:value=") + 1), 1, """");';
```

OpenOffice.org Version 2.0+:

```
PUT '            _offset = INDEX(_text, "office:currency=");';
PUT '            v[_count] = SCAN(SUBSTR(_text, _offset +
                              LENGTH("office:currency=") + 1),
                              1, """");';
PUT '            _offset = INDEX(_text, "office:value=");';
PUT '            v[_count] = TRIM(v[_count]) !!
                           SCAN(SUBSTR(_text, _offset +
                           LENGTH("office:value=") + 1), 1,
""");';

PUT '         END;';
PUT '         WHEN ("float", "percentage") DO;';
```

OpenOffice.org Version 1.1:

```
PUT '            _offset = INDEX(_text, "table:value=");';
PUT '            v[_count] = SCAN(SUBSTR(_text, _offset +
                              LENGTH("table:value=") + 1),
```

OpenOffice.org Version 2.0+:

```
PUT '          _offset = INDEX(_text, "office:value=");';
PUT '          v[_count] = SCAN(SUBSTR(_text, _offset +
                                  LENGTH("office:value=") + 1),

                                 1, """");';
PUT '          END;';
PUT '          OTHERWISE;';
PUT '        END;';
PUT '      END;';
PUT '    END;';
PUT '    ELSE IF _level = 4 AND
               _first NE 1 AND
               _last NE 1 THEN DO;';
PUT '    IF NOT (_type IN ("time", "date", "float",
                          "percentage", "currency")) then
           v[_count] = TRIM(v[_count]) !! TRIM(_text);';
PUT '    END;';
FILE __src(_output.source);
PUT '  IF _level = 3 AND _last = 1 THEN DO;';
PUT '    IF _repeat > 1 THEN DO _i = 1 TO (_repeat - 1);';
PUT '      _count + 1;';
PUT '      v[_count] = v[_count - 1];';
PUT '    END;';
PUT '    SELECT (PUT(_record, rngtab.));';
FILE __src(_run.source);
    PUT '        OTHERWISE;';
    PUT '      END;';
    PUT '    END;';
    PUT 'RUN;';
  END;
  j = TRIM(LEFT(PUT(_columns, 16.)));
  FILE __src(_data.source);
  PUT '    WORK.' _table '(KEEP = var1-var' j +(-1) ')';
  FILE __src(_output.source);
  PUT '        WHEN ("' _table +(-1) '") OUTPUT WORK.' _table
';';
RUN;
%INCLUDE __src(_data.source, _process.source,
               _output.source, _run.source) / SOURCE2;
```

5.5 Writing Data to Compatible Files for Spreadsheets

SAS/ACCESS for PC Files can be used to create individual worksheets directly for Excel and 1-2-3 spreadsheet software using PROC EXPORT. However, there are a number of alternative techniques that can be used without any requirements for a SAS/ACCESS license.

The following sections describe the techniques used to save data from SAS data sets into compatible files, which can then be read using your installed spreadsheet applications. The limitations of each technique are detailed and discussed.

5.5.1 Delimited Flat Files

In the following examples, the comma-separated files being created all have the suffix '**.csv**', which can be read successfully into Excel, Lotus 1-2-3, OpenOffice.org, and most database applications using the File ▶ Open menu options. Note that if their suffixes are changed to '**.xls**', Excel and OpenOffice.org 1.1 can read these files directly as if they were Excel spreadsheets, but Lotus 1-2-3 will give an error message of 'Untranslatable Excel file', because it must be informed of the internal data type before it can be read successfully. OpenOffice.org 2.0, prior to 2.0.2, opens the file as a text file.

The following SAS code will create the sample data for the following examples:

```
DATA exporting;
  SET sashelp.class;
  IF name = 'Thomas' THEN name = 'Tom, Jr';
  large = _N_ * 100;
  somedate = '16sep2003'D + _N_;
  anotherdate = somedate;
  textnumber = PUT(age, Z8.);
  FORMAT large COMMA8. somedate DATE9. anotherdate DDMMYY10.;
RUN;
```

Example 5.5 Using PROC EXPORT

The following example uses PROC EXPORT to create a comma-separated file with the first row containing variable names. All values are written as formatted values using their default SAS formats. Individual text values containing commas are quoted, but all other values are unquoted.

```
PROC EXPORT DATA = exporting
             FILE = 'export.csv'
             DBMS = CSV
             REPLACE;
RUN;
```

Caution: This technique does not guarantee that the data will be imported correctly as the intended text and numeric values, if any text values contains only numeric digits and no commas, or any numeric values are formatted with commas.

Example 5.6 Using ODS Statements

The following example uses the ODS CSV statements that were introduced as experimental in SAS 8.2. PROC PRINT is used to generate a simple record format with the third row in SAS 8.2, or the first row in SAS 9, containing quoted variable names, and subsequent records containing quoted values.

```
ODS LISTING CLOSE;
ODS CSV FILE = 'export.csv';
PROC PRINT DATA = exporting NOOBS;
  TITLE ' ';  * remove any existing titles *;
RUN;

ODS CSV CLOSE;
ODS LISTING;
```

The following example uses the ODS CSVALL statements that were also introduced as experimental in SAS 8.2. PROC PRINT is used to generate a simple record format with the third row in SAS 8.2 and SAS 9, containing quoted variable names, and subsequent records containing quoted values.

```
ODS LISTING CLOSE;
ODS CSVALL FILE = 'export.csv';

PROC PRINT DATA = exporting NOOBS;
  TITLE ' ';  * remove any existing titles *;
RUN;
ODS CSVALL CLOSE;
ODS LISTING;
```

Caution: This technique forces all values, whether text or numeric, to be imported as text values. All values are written as formatted values using their default SAS formats.

Example 5.7 Using Explicit PUT Statements in a DATA Step

If you know all the variable names in the SAS data set you want to export as a delimited flat file, then this technique is useful for creating suitable files for importing into spreadsheets and databases. The following example assumes that there are both text and numeric variables in the SAS data set, and that there is no requirement for variable names to be included as the first record. All the records contain quoted text values and unquoted numeric values, and all values are written as unformatted values.

```
DATA _NULL_;
  SET exporting;
  ARRAY _char {*} _CHARACTER_;  * include all text variables *;
  ARRAY _num {*} _NUMERIC_;  * include all numeric variables *;
  LENGTH _chartemp $200;  * sufficient to hold any text value
*;
  FILE 'export.csv';
  DO i = 1 TO DIM(_char);
    _chartemp = _char(i);
    PUT '"' _chartemp +(-1) '",' @;
  END;
  DO i = 1 TO DIM(_num);
    _numtemp = _num(i);
    PUT _numtemp +(-1) ',' @;
  END;
  PUT +(-1) ' ';  * to remove the final ',' *;
RUN;
```

Caution: This technique ensures that the data will probably be imported correctly as the intended text and numeric values. However, dates and times are written as internal SAS values that may not be interpreted in the same way when imported into spreadsheets and databases.

Table 5.2 Importing Comma-Separated Values into Spreadsheets and Databases

Application	"xxx"	"123"	xxx	123	11/08/03	11Aug2003	"11/08/03"	"11Aug2003"
Microsoft Excel	text	num	text	num	date	date	date	date
Lotus 1-2-3	text	text	text	num	date	text	text	text
OpenOffice.org	text	num	text	num	date	date	date	date
Microsoft Access	text	text	text	num	date	text	text	text
Lotus Approach	text	text	text	text	text	text	text	text

5.5.2 HTML Files

In the following example, the HTML file being created has the suffix '**.html**', which can be read successfully by Excel, Lotus 1-2-3, OpenOffice.org, and some database applications. Note that if the suffix is changed to '**.xls**', Excel and OpenOffice.org 1.1 can read the file directly as if it were an Excel spreadsheet, but Lotus 1-2-3 will give an error message of 'Untranslatable Excel file', because it must be informed of the internal data type before it can be read successfully. OpenOffice.org 2.0, prior to 2.0.2, opens the file as a text file.

Example 5.8 Using ODS HTML Statements

The following example uses the ODS HTML statements that were introduced in SAS 7. PROC PRINT is used to generate a simple HTML table containing formatted values.

```
ODS LISTING CLOSE;
ODS HTML FILE = 'report.html';

PROC PRINT DATA = exporting;
RUN;

ODS HTML CLOSE;
ODS LISTING;
```

Caution: This technique does not guarantee that the data will be imported correctly as the intended text and numeric values. In particular, any text values containing only numeric digits will be imported as numeric values. Dates formatted with the DDMMYY, MMDDYY, or YYMMDD formats will be imported correctly, although dates formatted with the DATE format may be imported as text.

Example 5.9 Using ODS MARKUP Statements to Generate Compact HTML

The following example uses the ODS MARKUP TAGSET=CHTML statements that were introduced in SAS 9. PROC PRINT is used to generate a simple HTML table containing formatted values, where the numeric data is right-justified and character data is left-justified in the columns.

```
ODS LISTING CLOSE;
ODS MARKUP TAGSET=CHTML FILE = 'report.html';

PROC PRINT DATA = exporting;
RUN;

ODS MARKUP CLOSE;
ODS LISTING;
```

Caution: This technique does not guarantee that the data will be imported correctly as the intended text and numeric values. In particular, any text values containing only numeric digits will be imported as numeric values. Dates formatted with the DDMMYY, MMDDYY, or YYMMDD formats will be corrected imported correctly, although dates formatted with the DATE format may be imported as text.

Example 5.10 Using ODS Statements and Forcing Text Values To Be Read As Text

The following example uses the same ODS HTML statements as in Example 5.8, but prefixes the all numeric text value with a '#' character to force it to be imported as a text value.

```
DATA temp (DROP = textnumber);
  SET exporting;
  textnumber2 = '#' !! textnumber;
RUN;

ODS LISTING CLOSE;
ODS HTML FILE = 'report.html';

PROC PRINT DATA = temp;
RUN;

ODS HTML CLOSE;
ODS LISTING;
```

Caution: This technique does not guarantee that the data will be imported correctly as the intended text and numeric values, unless a value has been explicitly prepared. As before, any text values still containing only numeric digits will be imported as numeric values. Dates formatted with the DDMMYY, MMDDYY, or YYMMDD formats will be corrected imported, although dates formatted with the DATE format may be imported as text.

It should also be noted that HTML files generated using ODS HTML statements can be very large compared with the original SAS data sets, e.g.:

Table 5.3 Comparison of Output File Sizes

File	Size in Kilobytes
sashelp.class	5.00
ODS LISTING with PROC PRINT DATA=sashelp.class	1.54
ODS HTML STYLE=default with PROC PRINT DATA=sashelp.class	23.20
ODS HTML STYLE=minimal with PROC PRINT DATA=sashelp.class	5.97
ODS MARKUP TAGSET=CHTML with PROC PRINT DATA=sashelp.class	3.03

It is recommended where the formatting is less important than the size of the HTML file that ODS MARKUP TAGSET=CHTML be used instead of ODS HTML.

Table 5.4 Importing HTML Table Values into Spreadsheets and Databases

Application	xxx	123	11/08/03	11Aug2003
Microsoft Excel	text	num	date	date
Lotus 1-2-3	text	num	date	text
OpenOffice.org	text	num	date	date
Microsoft Access	text	num	date	text

5.6 Converting Date and Time Formats

The following examples show data items containing date and/or time information, and suggestions for SAS code and formats to convert them to SAS dates, SAS times, or SAS datetime values:

Table 5.5 Date and Time Examples

Extract Data Examples	Sample SAS Code for Conversion
----+----1----+ 16May2003	(1) INPUT d DATE9.;
----+----1----+ 16 May 03	(1) INPUT d DATE9.;
----+----1----+ 16-May-2003	(1) INPUT d DATE11.;
----+----1----+ 16/05/2003	(1) INPUT d DDMMYY10.;
----+----1----+ 05/16/2003	(1) INPUT d MMDDYY10.;
----+----1----+ 2003/05/16	(1) INPUT d YYMMDD10.;
----+----1----+ 06/06/2003	(1) INPUT d DDMMYY10.; (2) INPUT d MMDDYY10.;
----+----1----+ 03/04/05	(1) INPUT d DDMMYY8.; (2) INPUT d MMDDYY8.; (3) INPUT d YYMMDD8.;
----+----1----+ 030405	(1) INPUT d DDMMYY6.; (2) INPUT d MMDDYY6.; (3) INPUT d YYMMDD6.;
----+----1----+ 2003-05-16	(1) INPUT d YYMMDD10.;
----+----1----+ 20030516	(1) INPUT d YYMMDD8.;
----+----1----+ May03	(1) INPUT d MONYY5.;
----+----1----+ 2003136	(1) INPUT d JULIAN7.;
----+----1----+ 99359	(1) INPUT d JULIAN5.;
----+----1 (hex digits) 2003136F	(1) INPUT t PDTIME4.; (2) INPUT t RMFDUR4.; (3) INPUT d PDJULG4.;
----+----1 (hex digits) 0103136F	(1) INPUT t PDTIME4.; (2) INPUT t RMFDUR4.; (3) INPUT d PDJULI4.;

Table 5.5 (*continued*)

Extract Data Examples	Sample SAS Code for Conversion
----+----1----+----2 (hex digits)0222307F0103136F	(1) `INPUT dt RMFSTAMP8.;`
----+----1----+----2 (hex digits)0103136F22230720	(1) `INPUT dt SHRSTAMP8.;`
----+----1----+----2 (hex digits)007AF7600103136F	(1) `INPUT dt SMFSTAMP8.;`
----+----1----+----2 (hex digits)B361183D5FB80000	(1) `INPUT dt TODSTAMP8.;`

A list of date and time informats for SAS 8 and SAS 9 are given here:

Table 5.6 Date Informats (SAS 8)

Date Informats (SAS 8)	Function (Date Values)	Input Data Examples	
DATE*w*.	Reads date values in the form **ddmmmyy** or **ddmmmyyyy**	`INPUT d DATE11.;` ----+----1----+ 16may03 16 may 2003 16-may-2003	15841 15841 15841
DDMMYY*w*.	Reads date values in the form **ddmmyy** or **ddmmyyyy**	`INPUT d DDMMYY10.;` ----+----1----+ 160503 16/05/2003 16 05 2003	15841 15841 15841

EURDFDE*w*.	Reads international date values	`OPTIONS DFLANG=SPANISH;`
		`INPUT d EURDFDE10.;`
		----+----1----+
		15abr2003
		15-abr-03
			15810
			15810

EURDFMY*w*.	Reads month and year date values in the form **mmmyy** or **mmmyyyy**	`OPTIONS DFLANG=FRENCH;`
		`INPUT d EURDFMY7.;`
		----+----1
		avr2003
		avr 03
			15796
			15796

(continued)

Table 5.6 (*continued*)

Date Informats (SAS 8)	Function (Date Values)	Input Data Examples	

JULIAN*w*.	Reads Julian dates in the form **yyddd** or **yyyyddd**	`INPUT d JULIAN7.;`
		`----+----1`
		`99359`
		`2003125`
			1460
			15830

MINGUO*w*.	Reads dates in Taiwanese form	`INPUT d MINGUO10.;`
		`----+----1----+`
		`92/05/16`
		`920516`
		`92-05-16`
			15841
			15841
			15841

MMDDYY*w*.	Reads date values in the form **mmddyy** or **mmddyyyy**	`INPUT d MMDDYY10.;`
		`----+----1----+`
		`051603`
		`05/16/2003`
		`05 16 2003`
			15841
			15841
			15841

MONYY*w*.	Reads month and year date values in the form **mmmyy** or **mmmyyyy**	`INPUT d MONYY7.;`
		`----+----1`
		`may 03`
		`may2003`
			15826
			15826

NENGO*w*.	Reads Japanese date values in the form **eyymmdd**	`INPUT d NENGO10.;`
		`----+----1----+`
		`H.150516`
		`H150516`
		`15/05/16`
			15841
			15841
			15841

PDJULG*w*.	Reads packed Julian date values in the hexadecimal form **yyyyddd**F for IBM	`INPUT d PDJULG4.;`
		`----+----1 (hex digits)`
		`1999359F`
		`2003125F`
			14603
			15830

PDJULI*w*.	Reads packed Julian dates in the hexadecimal format **ccyyddd**F for IBM	`INPUT d PDJULI4.;`
		`----+----1 (hex digits)`
		`0099359F`
		`0103125F`
			14603
			15830

YYMMDD*w*.	Reads date values in the form **yymmdd** or **yyyymmdd**	`INPUT d YYMMDD10.;`
		`----+----1----+`
		`031605`
		`2003/16/05`
		`2003 16 05`
			15841
			15841
			15841

YYMMN*w*.	Reads date values in the form **yyyymm** or **yymm**	`INPUT d YYMMN6.;`
		`----+----1`
		`0305`
		`200305`
			15826
			15826

Table 5.6 (*continued*)

Date Informats (SAS 8)	Function (Date Values)	Input Data Examples
YYQw.	Reads quarters of the year	``` INPUT d YYQ9.; ----+----1 03Q2 15796 03Q02 15796 2003Q02 15796 2003Q2 15796 ```
DATETIMEw.	Reads datetime values in the form **ddmmmyy hh:mm:ss.ss** or **ddmmmyyyy hh:mm:ss.ss**	``` INPUT dt DATETIME20.; ----+----1----+----2 16may03:22:23:07.2 1368742987.2 16may2003/22:23:07.2 1368742987.2 16may2003/10:23 PM 1368742980.0 ```
EURDFDTw.	Reads international datetime values in the form **ddmmmyy hh:mm:ss.ss** or **ddmmmyyyy hh:mm:ss.ss**	``` OPTIONS DFLANG=GERMAN; INPUT dt EURDFDT20.; ----+----1----+----2 16mai03:22:23:07.2 1368742987.2 16mai2003:22:23:07.2 1368742987.2 ```
RMFSTAMPw.	Reads time and date fields of RMF records	``` INPUT dt RMFSTAMP8.; ----+----1----+----2 (hex digits) 0222307F0103136F 1368742987.0 ```
SHRSTAMPw.	Reads date and time values of SHR records	``` INPUT dt SHRSTAMP8.; ----+----1----+----2 (hex digits) 0103136F22230720 1368742987.2 ```
SMFSTAMPw.	Reads time and date values of SMF records	``` INPUT dt SMFSTAMP8.; ----+----1----+----2 (hex digits) 007AF7600103136F 1368742987.2 ```
TODSTAMPw.	Reads an eight-byte time-of-day stamp	``` INPUT dt TODSTAMP8.; ----+----1----+----2 (hex digits) B361183D5FB80000 1262303998.0 ```

Table 5.7 Time Informats (SAS 8)

Time Informats (SAS 8)	Function (Time Values)	Input Data Examples

MSEC*w*.	Reads TIME MIC values	`INPUT t MSEC8.;`
		`----+----1----+----2` (hex digits)
		`0000EA044E65A000` `62818.412122`

PDTIME*w*.	Reads packed decimal time of SMF and RMF records	`INPUT t PDTIME4.;`
		`----+----1` (hex digits)
		`0222307F` `80587.0`

RMFDUR*w*.	Reads duration intervals of RMF records	`INPUT t RMFDUR4.;`
		`----+----1` (hex digits)
		`2307200F` `1387.2`

TIME*w*.	Reads hours, minutes, and seconds in the form **hh:mm:ss.ss**	`INPUT t TIME10.;`
		`----+----1----+`
		`22:23:07` `80587.0`
		`10:23 PM` `80580.0`

TU*w*.	Reads timer units	`INPUT t TU8.;`
		`----+----1----+----2` (hex digits)
		`8FC7A9BC` `62818.412122`

Table 5.8 Date and Time Informats (SAS 9)

Date and Time Informats (SAS 9)	Function	Input Data Examples

ANYDTDTE*w*.	Reads and converts a variety of date values	`OPTIONS DATESTYLE=DMY;`
		`INPUT d ANYDTDTE12.;`
		`----+----1----+`
		`16may2003` `15841`
		`16/05/2003` `15841`
		`05/16/2003` `15841`
		`2003/05/16` `15841`
		`May2003` `15826`
		`2003Q2` `15796`
		`2003-May-16` `15841`
		`May 16, 2003` `15841`
		`May 16 2003` `15841`
		`2003125` `15830`
		`20030516` `15841`

Table 5.8 (*continued*)

Date and Time Informats (SAS 9)	Function	Input Data Examples
ANYDTDTM*w*.	Reads and converts a variety of datetime values	OPTIONS DATESTYLE=DMY; INPUT dt ANYDTDTM20.; ----+----1----+----2 16MAY2003:22:23:07 1368742987.0 2003/05/16:22:23:07 1368742987.0
ANYDTTME*w*.	Reads and converts a variety of time values	INPUT t ANYDTTME7.; ----+----1 22:23:07 80587 10:23 PM 80580

5.7 Summary

5.7.1 Importing

- Using database backup files minimizes the impact of SAS processes on production databases.
- $EBCDIC and S370FF informats are required to read IBM mainframe data into SAS on other platforms.
- It is sometimes better to force the reading of all data into SAS as text, then converting selected items to numeric, dates or time values later, because it simplifies the import processing.
- Date and time data can be stored in extract files in a wide variety of forms, depending on the source, usage, and location, so the informat used to read each data item needs to be carefully selected.

5.7.2 Exporting

- Data suitable for importing into spreadsheet or database applications can be generated as delimited text by using PROC EXPORT, or HTML files by using ODS.

- Quoting and formatting of the exported data from SAS can affect the way data is imported into other applications.

5.8 Recommended Reading

For more information, go to www.hollandnumerics.com/books/Saving_Time_and_Money_using_SAS.htm. This page includes a chapter-by-chapter list of recommended reading.

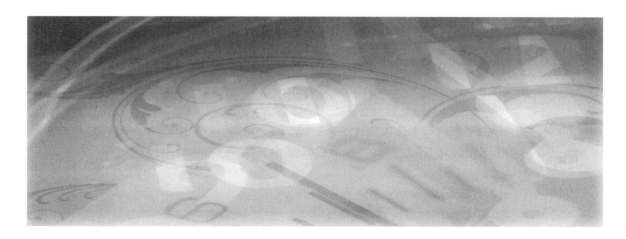

Chapter 6

Developing SAS Applications Using SAS Enterprise Guide

6.1 Abstract

The bundling of SAS Enterprise Guide 3.0 and 4.1 with SAS 9 for Windows has introduced a much greater number of users to this thin-client front end to SAS. Using a thin client, rather than SAS on a PC, to develop SAS applications requires different techniques to get the best out of the new environment. This chapter discusses a number of features of SAS Enterprise Guide that can assist both novice and experienced SAS developers. It also describes a case study involving the introduction of SAS Enterprise Guide and SAS software to a new client site.

6.2 Introduction to SAS Enterprise Guide

6.2.1 What Is SAS Enterprise Guide?

Throughout this chapter, SAS Enterprise Guide should be assumed to be 4.1, unless otherwise stated, and being run on a Windows XP Professional SP2 platform. The remote servers mentioned were installed on GNU/Linux Mandriva 2006, Debian/Linux Ubuntu 6.10, or UNIX Solaris 8 platforms.

SAS Enterprise Guide is a Windows-only thin-client application that uses the Microsoft .NET and Data Access Components to communicate with the SAS Integration Technologies component. While access to SAS installations on remote Windows, Linux, or UNIX platforms requires SAS Integration Technologies to be licensed on that system, SAS Enterprise Guide can act as a front end to a locally installed SAS system, referred to as the local server, even if only Base SAS has been licensed.

The thin-client architecture enables users to access data and run data processing tasks on the server, but develop the tasks in a familiar local environment on the PC. Only the code and results are transmitted between the PC and server.

Figure 6.1 Client Server Architecture

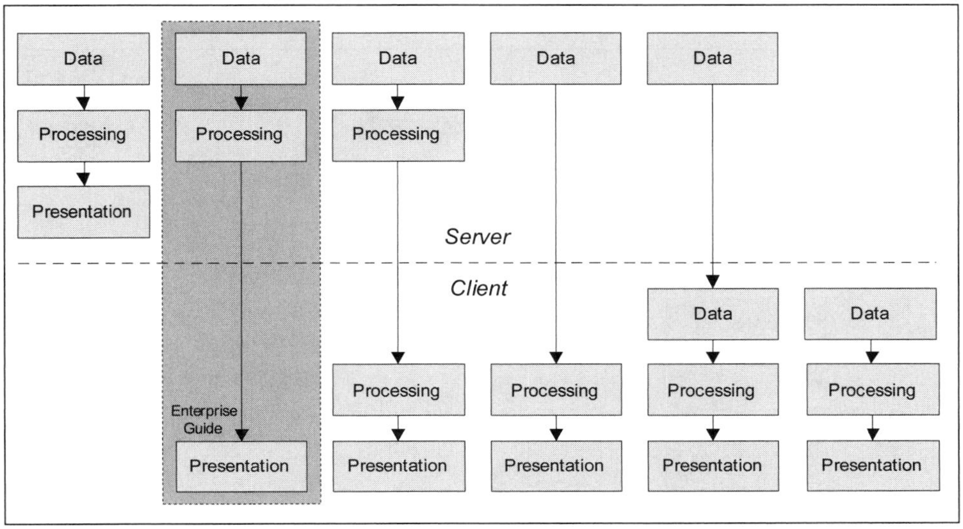

6.2.2 Limitations of SAS Enterprise Guide

- Because SAS Enterprise Guide acts as an editor and batch scheduler for separate SAS systems, it cannot be used to run SAS applications that have their own GUIs or interactive features, e.g., SAS/AF, SAS/EIS, SAS/INSIGHT, SAS/ASSIST, SAS/GIS, SAS/SPECTRAVIEW, etc. All processes should be considered to be batch jobs, in that they have no interactive facilities. However, the SAS code is actually running in a single SAS session on the selected SAS server, so from the first code submission, WORK data sets, option settings, and macro variables are retained until the end of the server session, or until they are manually deleted.

- The batch SAS processes can return only the following items back to SAS Enterprise Guide:
  SAS log
  SAS output via ODS
  SAS graphs

- Although the SAS Enterprise Guide user interface includes elements relating to Base SAS, SAS/STAT, SAS/GRAPH, SAS/ETS, and SAS/QC, their applicability will depend on the SAS license installed on the SAS server selected to run the code.

- SAS Enterprise Guide cannot directly read SAS catalog entries.

Figure 6.2 Software Requirements for Local and Remote Servers

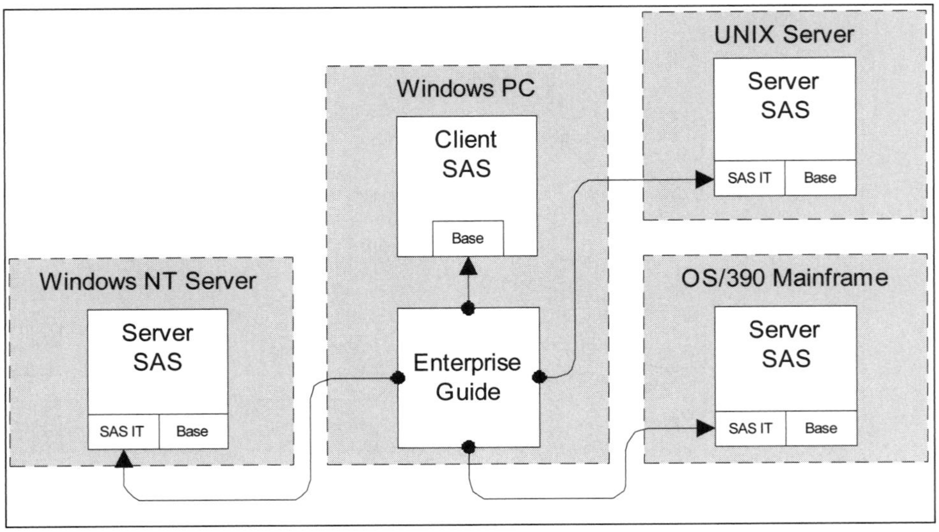

6.2.3 User Interface

The GUI consists of an equivalent of the Results window (called the Project window), a desktop for displaying the equivalents of the Log and Output windows, and a Task Status window.

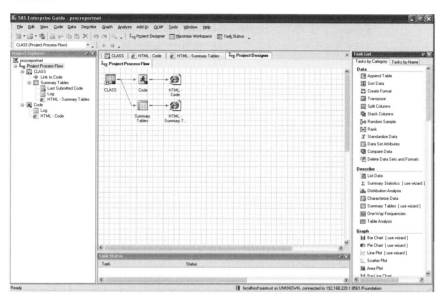

There is also a Task List, which includes a list of facilities to generate SAS code for most of the commonly used procedures in Base SAS, SAS/STAT, SAS/GRAPH, SAS/ETS, and SAS/QC without any need to be able to write SAS code by hand. However, if you want to use tasks that use components other than Base SAS locally or remotely, then you must have a license for these components on the local or remote server where the SAS code will be run.

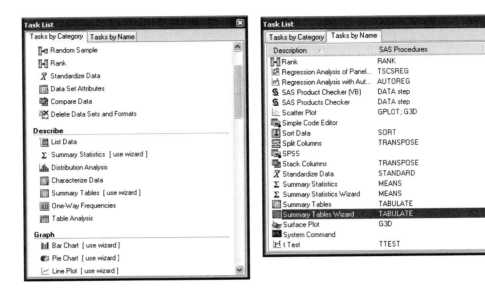

However, if there is a need to write SAS code by hand, or to enhance the code that was generated by SAS Enterprise Guide, then the Code window is available, which uses the SAS Enhanced Editor ActiveX add-in.

By default, task, code, and data entries are grouped together in Projects, which can be saved to disk as *.egp files. Projects were stored by SAS Enterprise Guide 2.0 as *.seg files, which, when opened in SAS Enterprise Guide 4.1, are automatically converted to SAS Enterprise Guide 4.0 Projects. These files can be saved on the local PC, on a network-connected disk, or on any SAS server connected via SAS Enterprise Guide. Project entries can be viewed in the Project Explorer window or the Project Designer window.

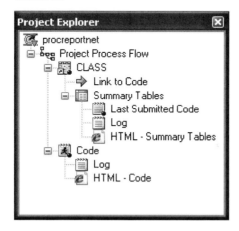 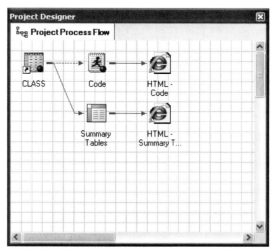

SAS data sets, or links to SAS data sets, are stored in data entries. A wide range of other file types can be converted to or from SAS data sets, e.g., Excel spreadsheets, Access database tables, and delimited and fixed-column flat files.

For example, importing data into SAS data sets:

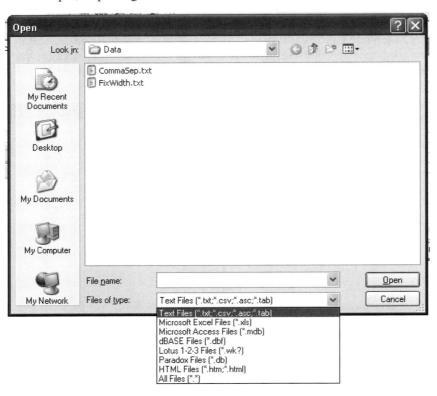

For example, exporting data from SAS data sets:

6.2.4 Tasks

The tasks, which provide facilities to generate SAS code for most of the commonly used procedures, are used via a point-and-click interface. Information about files, data sets, data columns, and options is shown, and can be set, in task-specific dialog boxes.

Some of the tasks, e.g., Summary Tables, employ skeleton diagrams that the user can populate, using drag-and-drop actions, to build the required report layout.

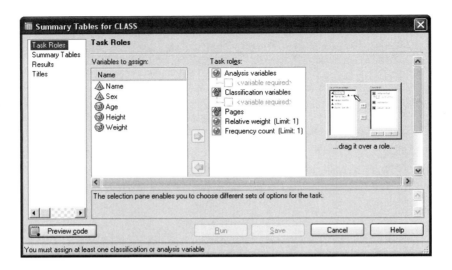

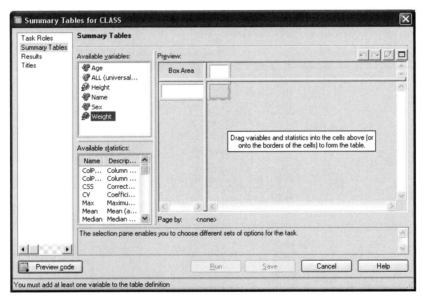

The tasks are not intended to cover 100% of the functionality of the corresponding SAS procedure, but they will generate SAS code for the commonly used features.

It should be noted that, because the thin-client architecture has no direct access to SAS until the task is finally run, it is possible to generate SAS code for unlicensed SAS components, which will fail as a consequence. While the list of tasks can be customized to omit entries relating to unlicensed components, this may not be appropriate if several servers with differing licenses can be accessed.

6.2.5 Traditional Programming

Most generated SAS code can be previewed and copied into other programs, helping novice users develop their programming skills by example, and reminding more experienced programmers of relevant, but infrequently used, syntax.

```
Code Preview for Task                                                  ⊠
  Insert Code...

 /* ------------------------------------------------------------
       Run the tabulate procedure
     ------------------------------------------------------------ */
⊟PROC TABULATE
  DATA=SASHELP.CLASS

        ;
     VAR Weight Height;
     CLASS Name /    ORDER=UNFORMATTED MISSING;
     CLASS Sex / ORDER=UNFORMATTED MISSING;
     CLASS Age / ORDER=UNFORMATTED MISSING;
     TABLE /* Row Dimension */
 Age,
 /* Column Dimension */
 Sex*(
   Height*
     Mean
   Weight*
     Mean)        ;
     ;

 RUN;
 /* ------------------------------------------------------------
     End of task code.
     ------------------------------------------------------------ */
 RUN; QUIT;
```

The copied SAS code can then be manually edited in a Code window to include additional features not generated by the GUI.

6.3 Hints and Tips for SAS Enterprise Guide Administrators

6.3.1 Accessing Local SAS Installations

SAS Enterprise Guide can be used as a point-and-click front end to a locally installed SAS system. This requires client SAS software to be installed on the Windows system, including the local version of SAS Integration Technologies, which is supplied as part of Base SAS. The only SAS component that must be licensed is Base SAS.

Accessing the locally installed SAS system may require it to be registered using the **-REGSERVER** option on SAS.EXE, if the installation has not been installed to the default location, or if several different versions have been installed on the same PC. For automated installations it is recommended that this registration be carried out even if the location is the default.

6.3.2 Accessing Server-Based SAS Installations

A remote SAS server requires only Base SAS and SAS Integration Technologies to be installed and licensed in order to be accessed, although if SAS/STAT, SAS/GRAPH, SAS/ETS, and SAS/QC are installed and licensed on the server, then they can have code generated for them by SAS Enterprise Guide using standard tasks. Other components can also be used, but will require direct coding in a SAS Code node to be executed from SAS Enterprise Guide.

The remote SAS server must be configured using the SAS Enterprise Guide Explorer, which can be accessed from SAS Enterprise Guide by selecting **Tools ▶ SAS Enterprise Guide Explorer**. New servers can be added using the Server Wizard, which can be started from inside the SAS Enterprise Guide Explorer by selecting **File ▶ New ▶ Server**. Each new server definition requires the following information: server name (user-defined, but must be unique), connection protocol (probably IOM), host address (either URL or IP address), and port number of the object spawner on the remote server.

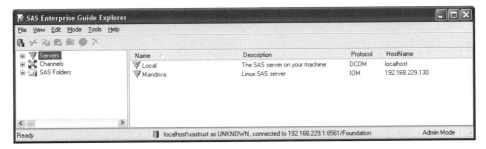

6.3.3 Why You Cannot Use Autoexec.sas

SAS Enterprise Guide communicates with SAS via a special interface component called SAS Integration Technologies. Because the requests for SAS functionality are typically small and frequent, starting a full SAS session each time would be wasteful, and probably too slow. As a consequence, SAS Integration Technologies starts only a minimal system that can be extended, if required, as the code is compiled. This minimal system does not include any autoexec processing, so any processing required to be carried out prior to each request must be initiated using the **-INITSTMT** option. Therefore, the following option is equivalent to the **-AUTOEXEC** option:

```
-INITSTMT '%INCLUDE "/home/user/autoexec.sas;"'
```

When using the SAS Enterprise Guide Administrator, this **-INITSTMT** option is specified during the server setup screens by typing the following text in the SAS startup statements box on the Options tab:

```
%INCLUDE "/home/user/autoexec.sas";
```

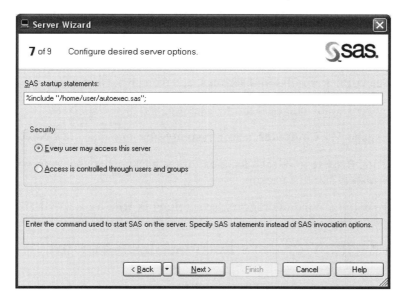

As an alternative, the **-INITSTMT** option can be added to the **-sasCommand** option in the SAS Object Spawner configuration file.

6.3.4 Why Do Platform-Specific System Commands Fail?

The starting parameters on the SAS Object Spawners that start the SAS server sessions can have an impact on the permitted functionality of the SAS code submitted to run on the server. Statements such as **X**, **%SYSEXEC**, **SYSTASK**, and **CALL SYSTEM**, the **SYSTEM** function, and the **FILENAME** option **PIPE** will not work unless the **-ALLOWXCMD** or **-NONOXCMD** parameters are explicitly added to the SAS Object Spawner configuration. However, the use of these options should be permitted only with great caution, because other platform-specific operating system commands can also be submitted from submitted SAS code, which could be dangerous when used by inexperienced or malicious users!

Note that even if you run your SAS code only on the local server, you will not be able to use statements such as **X**, **%SYSEXEC**, **SYSTASK**, and **CALL SYSTEM**, the **SYSTEM** function, and the **FILENAME** option **PIPE**, unless you have allowed operating system commands. The local server parameters are stored in the Windows registry and can be changed as follows (after a backup of the Windows registry has been taken, because any manual updates of the registry can affect the operation of Windows):

1. To back up the Windows registry, select **Start ▶ All Programs ▶ Accessories ▶ System Tools ▶ Backup**.

2. Select **Back up files and settings**, and then click **Next**.

3. Select **Let me choose what to back up**, and then click **Next**.

4. Expand **My Computer**, select **System State**, and then click **Next**.

5. Click **Browse** to select a location for the backup, and then select **Save Next ▶ Finish** to start the backup.

6. To edit the Windows registry, select **Start ▶ Run**, type REGEDIT, and then click **OK**.

7. Select **HKEY_CLASSES_ROOT with CLSID=440196D4**, and then click the **LocalServer32** key.

8. Right-click **Default**, and then click **Modify**.

9. Remove "**-noxcmd**", which should be the last item in the list, and then click **OK**.

10. Select **View Refresh**.

11. Exit the Registry window.

6.3.5 Changing the Current Directory

When you start a SAS session, the current directory is always your home directory on the server platform, e.g., **c:\winnt\system32** on Windows, or **/home/***userid* on Linux or UNIX. To change the current directory to a different location, you need to have the ability to run operating system commands (see Section 6.3.4, "Why Do Platform-Specific System Commands Fail?". Any of the following techniques are applicable:

1. X statement

   On a Windows server:
   ```
   OPTIONS NOXSYNC NOXWAIT;
   X 'd:; cd d:\data\lib';
   ```

   On a Linux or UNIX server:
   ```
   OPTIONS NOXSYNC NOXWAIT;
   X 'cd /data/lib';
   ```

2. %SYSEXEC statement

   On a Windows server:
   ```
   OPTIONS NOXSYNC NOXWAIT;
   %SYSEXEC d:;
   %SYSEXEC cd d:\data\lib;
   ```

   On a Linux or UNIX server:
   ```
   %SYSEXEC cd /data/lib;
   ```

3. SYSTASK statement

   On a Windows server:
   ```
   OPTIONS NOXSYNC NOXWAIT;
   SYSTASK COMMAND 'd:; cd d:\data\lib';
   ```

   On a Linux or UNIX server:
   ```
   OPTIONS NOXSYNC NOXWAIT;
   SYSTASK COMMAND 'cd /data/lib';
   ```

4. CALL SYSTEM statement

   On a Windows server:
   ```
   OPTIONS NOXSYNC NOXWAIT;
   DATA _NULL_;
     CALL SYSTEM('d:; cd d:\data\lib');
   RUN;
   ```

On a Linux or UNIX server:
```
OPTIONS NOXSYNC NOXWAIT;
DATA _NULL_;
  CALL SYSTEM('cd /data/lib');
RUN;
```

5. SYSTEM function

On a Windows server:
```
OPTIONS NOXSYNC NOXWAIT;
DATA _NULL_;
  rc = SYSTEM('d:; cd d:\data\lib');
RUN;
```

On a Linux or UNIX server:
```
OPTIONS NOXSYNC NOXWAIT;
DATA _NULL_;
  rc = SYSTEM('cd /data/lib');
RUN;
```

6. FILENAME statement with the PIPE option

On a Windows server:
```
FILENAME cmd PIPE 'd:; cd d:\data\lib';
DATA _NULL_;
  INFILE cmd TRUNCOVER;
  INPUT;
  PUT _INFILE_;
RUN;
```

On a Linux or UNIX server:
```
FILENAME cmd PIPE 'cd /data/lib';
DATA _NULL_;
  INFILE cmd TRUNCOVER;
  INPUT;
  PUT _INFILE_;
RUN;
```

6.4 Hints and Tips for SAS Enterprise Guide Users

6.4.1 Installing SAS Enterprise Guide Custom Tasks

Using the Add-In Manager to Add a Custom Task and View the List of Available Custom Tasks

1. Open SAS Enterprise Guide and select the **Add-In** menu option.

2. Click the **Add-In Manager** option in the drop-down list.

3. Select **User** from the **Registry** list.

4. In the **Add-In** list, select the custom task you want to add.

5. Click the **Update** button.

6. If a window informs you that the registry will be modified, then click **OK**.

7. Click **OK** to close the **Add-In Manager** dialog box.

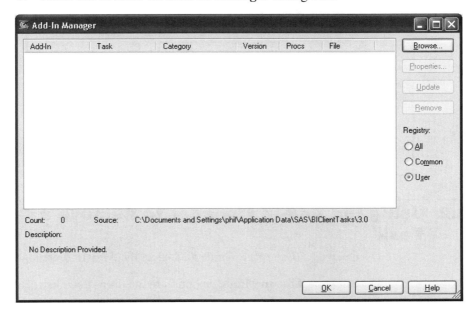

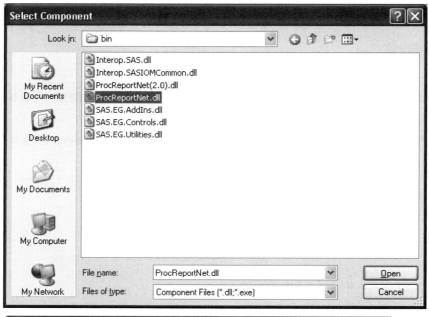

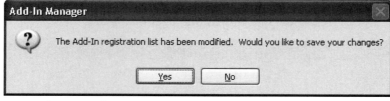

6.4.2 Using the Add-In Manager to Remove a Custom Task

1. Open SAS Enterprise Guide and select the **Add-In** menu option.

2. Click the **Add-In Manager** option in the drop-down list.

3. Select **User** from the **Registry** list.

4. In the **Add-In** list, select the custom task you want to remove.

5. Click the **Remove** button.

6. Click **OK** to close the Add-In Manager dialog box.

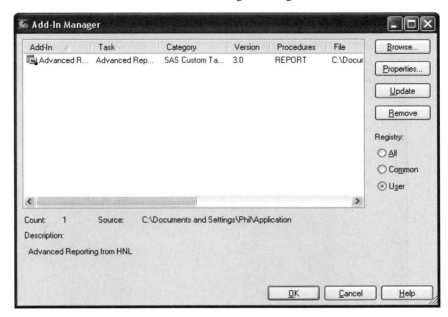

Using Windows Explorer to Add or Remove a Custom Task

There is another method of adding a custom task to SAS Enterprise Guide 4.1, which is to copy the DLL file to
C:\Program Files\SAS Institute\Shared Files\BIClientTasks\Custom (if SAS 8.2 was installed on the PC first), or
C:\Program Files\SAS\Shared Files\BIClientTasks\Custom (if SAS 9 was installed first). The custom task should be removed by deleting the copied file.

Caution: This method of adding custom tasks bypasses the functionality of the Add-In Manager, which will not be able to replace or remove any custom tasks added using this method, although these custom tasks may still be visible in the Add-In Manager windows.

A Sample Custom Task

The following screen shots were taken from a SAS Enterprise Guide custom task that I wrote to generate HTML-based reports using PROC REPORT. There are currently no built-in SAS Enterprise Guide tasks that will generate SAS code for PROC REPORT.

The first window enables the variables found in the active data set to be added to groups of variable types, which will determine how they will be added to the final report.

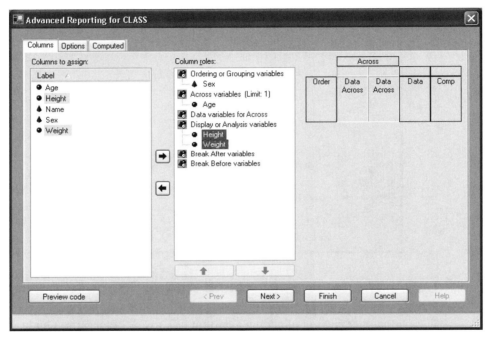

The next window is used to select the reporting options that are not specifically associated with any particular variable.

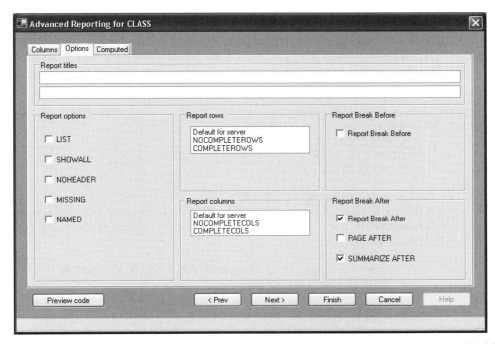

The final window is used to include the code for any computed columns to be added into the report.

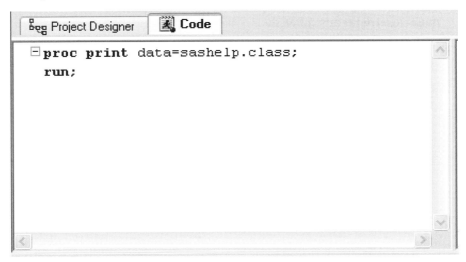

Sample code and information about developing your own SAS Enterprise Guide custom tasks can be found at **www.sas.com**.

Reading from and Writing to SAS Catalogs

While SAS catalog source entries cannot be edited directly, it is possible to use the CATALOG option of the FILENAME statement in the SAS code to read and write SOURCE entries in catalogs. For example, on a Linux or UNIX server:

```
FILENAME catsrc CATALOG 'lib.cat';
DATA _NULL_;
  INFILE catsrc(member.source);
  INPUT;
  FILE '/home/user/member.sas';
  PUT _INFILE_;
RUN;
```

On submitting this code, the contents of the SOURCE entry called Member are copied to the **member.sas** file in **/home/user**. Follow these instructions to edit the file in SAS Enterprise Guide:

1. From the main menu, select **Insert ▶ Code ▶ Existing ▶ /home/user/member.sas**.

2. Edit the text in the Code window.

3. Save the updated text by selecting a **File ▶ Export ▶ /home/user/editedmember.sas**.

The following SAS code will replace the existing SAS CATALOG entry with the text in **/home/user/editedmember.sas**:

```
FILENAME catsrc CATALOG 'lib.cat';
DATA _NULL_;
  INFILE '/home/user/editedmember.sas';
  INPUT;
  FILE catsrc(member.source);
  PUT _INFILE_;
RUN;
```

6.4.3 Generating SAS Code Using SAS Enterprise Guide Tasks

All the GUI tasks in SAS Enterprise Guide generate SAS code that can be submitted automatically, but using the Preview Code option gives the user an opportunity to copy the generated code prior to submission and paste it into a separate SAS Code node in SAS Enterprise Guide to edit and run later.

6.4.4 Scheduling Batch SAS Processes

Windows Local or Remote Servers

Batch processes can be scheduled to run at specific or regular times and dates using the Task Scheduler (via the **at** command) in Windows NT, 2000, or XP, provided the Task Scheduler service has been started either manually or automatically.

The **at** command syntax is as follows:

```
AT [\\computername] [ [id] [/DELETE] | /DELETE [/YES]]
AT [\\computername] time [/INTERACTIVE]
    [ /EVERY:date[,...] | /NEXT:date[,...]] "command"
```

The following table describes the **at** command options:

Table 6.1 Windows Command Options for at

Option	Description	Example
\\computername	Specifies a remote computer, either as a name or as an IP address. Commands are scheduled on the local computer if this parameter is omitted.	`\\server` `\\124.11.57.49`
id	Is an identification number assigned to a scheduled command, which is displayed when a task is scheduled, or is in the list displayed by the **at** command without any parameters.	`24`
/DELETE	Cancels a scheduled command. If id is omitted, all the scheduled commands on the computer are canceled.	`/delete`

(continued)

Table 6.1 (*continued*)

Option	Description	Example
/YES	Used with the cancel all jobs command when no further confirmation is desired.	/yes
time	Specifies the time when a command is to run.	21:30
/INTERACTIVE	Enables the job to interact with the desktop of the user who is logged on at the time the job runs.	/interactive
/EVERY:date[,...]	Runs the command on each specified day(s) of the week or month. Days of the week can be specified from the following list: Su, Mo, Tu, We, Th, Fr, Sa. Days of the month can be specified as any integer between 1 and 31. If the date is omitted, the current day of the month is assumed.	/every:Tu,Th,15
/NEXT:date[,...]	Runs the specified command on the next occurrence of the day (for example, next Thursday). Days of the week can be specified from the following list: Su, Mo, Tu, We, Th, Fr, Sa. Days of the month can be specified as any integer between 1 and 31. If the date is omitted, the current day of the month is assumed.	/next:We,Fr,19
"command"	Is the Windows command, or batch program to be run.	"start_pgm.cmd"

Here is an example of SAS Enterprise Guide code that could be used to schedule a batch process at 22:30:

```
FILENAME cmd PIPE 'at 22:30 c:\temp\startsas.cmd';
DATA _NULL_;
  INFILE cmd;
  INPUT;
  PUT _INFILE_;
RUN;
```

A SAS application to be run in the background can be started by including the following commands in the **startsas.cmd** file, which will process the code in **C:\temp\prog.sas**, and store the SAS log and SAS output in the same folder:

```
c:
cd temp
sas -input prog.sas -log prog.log -print prog.lst -batch -nologo
```

6.4.5 Linux or UNIX Remote Servers

Batch processes can be scheduled to run at specific or regular times and dates using the **at** and **batch** commands in Linux or UNIX, provided the scheduler daemon has been started either manually or automatically.

The **at** and **batch** commands syntax is as follows, where the **at** command sets a specific time for the command to be executed, and the **batch** command executes commands when system load levels permit; in other words, when the load average drops below 0.8:

```
at [-V] [-q queue] [-f file] [-mldv] TIME
at -c id [id [...]]
batch [-V] [-q queue] [-f file] [-mv] [TIME]
```

The **atq** command is used to display the currently scheduled commands:

```
atq [-V] [-q queue]
```

The **atrm** command is used to delete currently scheduled commands:

```
atrm [-V] id [id [...]]
```

The following table describes the command options:

Table 6.2 Linux or UNIX Command Options for at and batch

Option	Description	Example
-V	Displays the version number.	`-V`
-q queue	Uses the specified queue. A queue designation consists of a single letter; valid queue designations range from a to z. and A to Z. The a queue is the default for **at,** and the b queue is the default for **batch**. Queues with higher letters run with increased niceness. The special queue "=" is reserved for jobs that are currently running.	`-q m` `-q R`
-f file	Is the Linux or UNIX command, or batch program to be run.	`-f "startsas.sh"`
-m	Sends an e-mail to the user on completion, even if the command does not create any output.	`-m`
-l	Is an alias for the **atq** command.	`-l`
-d	Is an alias for the **atrm** command.	`-d`
-v	Displays the time the command will be executed.	`-v`

TIME	Accepts times of the form HH:MM to run a command at a specific time of day. If that time is already past, the next day is assumed. You may also specify midnight, noon, or teatime (4 p.m.), and you can have a time-of-day suffixed with AM or PM for running in the morning or the evening. You can also say what day the command will be run, by giving a date in the form month-day with an optional year, or giving a date of the form MMDDYY or MM/DD/YY or DD.MM.YY. The specification of a date must follow the specification of the time of day. You can also give times like now + count time-units, where the time-units can be minutes, hours, days, or weeks, and you can tell **at** to run the command today by suffixing the time with today and to run the command tomorrow by suffixing the time with tomorrow.	`21:30`
		`4pm + 3 days`
		`now`
		`midnight`
		`10:25 tomorrow`
		`13:05 25.12.04`

(continued)

Table 6.2 (*continued*)

Option	Description	Example
-c	Concatenates the scheduled command identifier(s) listed to the standard output.	`-c`
id	The identification number assigned to a scheduled command, which is displayed when a task is scheduled, or is in the list displayed by the **atq** command.	`24`

Here is an example of SAS Enterprise Guide code that could be used to schedule a batch process at 14:45:

```
FILENAME cmd PIPE 'at -f /home/user/startsas.sh 14:45';
DATA _NULL_;
  INFILE cmd;
  INPUT;
  PUT _INFILE_;
RUN;
```

A SAS application to be run in the background can be started by including the following commands in the **startsas.sh** file, which will process the code in **/home/user/prog.sas**, and store the SAS log and SAS output in the same folder:

```
cd /home/user
sas -input prog.sas -log prog.log -print prog.lst -batch -nologo
```

6.5 Introducing SAS Enterprise Guide at a New Client Site—A Case Study

6.5.1 Environment

SAS software was introduced into the risk management department in this finance company to process massive volumes of historical customer records in flat files, which were copied to a UNIX server from the mainframe.

Existing analysis tools located on their PCs used a combination of a Visual Basic extraction application, SPSS data processing, and Excel spreadsheets for reporting. The monthly data processing was carried out in a number of manual steps over a period of 2 weeks each month. The standard reports and charts then took an additional 2 weeks to produce.

Figure 6.3 Original Environment

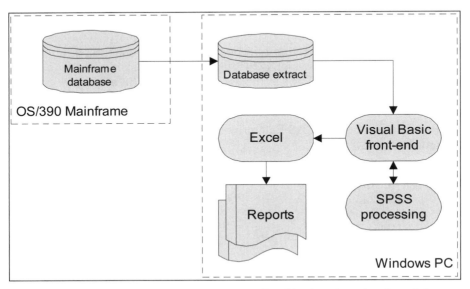

The new SAS data warehouse processed the flat files into location-based data marts on the UNIX server, which could then be queried using SAS code submitted from SAS Enterprise Guide on their PCs. The monthly data processing was carried out automatically over 2 days, usually over a weekend, and the standard reports were produced using SAS Enterprise Guide and Excel during the following 1½ to 2 weeks. This left an extra 2 weeks available each month to perform ad hoc queries on the stored data marts.

The individual data marts varied in size up to around 10 Gb for some specific locations, making the data transfer alone from server to PC impractical.

SAS Enterprise Guide provided the means to keep the data and the processing on the server, while still using the text editing and data viewing of the PC Windows environment.

Figure 6.4 New Environment with SAS Enterprise Guide

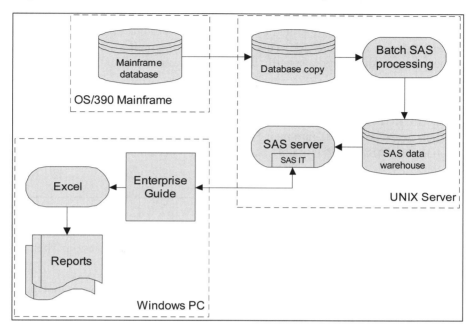

6.5.2 User Training

At the beginning of the project the users had SAS Enterprise Guide 1.1 and
Enterprise Reporter 2.5 installed on their PCs, and received SAS training in basic SAS
programming and introductions to SAS Enterprise Guide and SAS Enterprise Reporter.
The SAS server had SAS Integration Technologies, SAS/STAT, and SAS/ACCESS for
PC File Formats installed.

SAS Enterprise Reporter was intended to provide the users with graphical reports, but it
lacked the charting capabilities they had been used to in Excel.

In SAS Enterprise Guide 1.1 the Query task built SAS views, rather than SAS data sets,
for each extract, causing unnecessarily long response times when querying the larger data
marts. Fortunately, these issues were resolved in SAS Enterprise Guide 1.3, which
dramatically increased its usability.

In general, the users did not use the GUIs to submit code, partly because of their
experiences with SAS Enterprise Guide 1.1. Instead the GUIs were used to generate code
in the correct syntax, which was then copied from the Preview window into the programs
they were developing.

Although SAS Enterprise Guide generated reports by default as Web pages, the users continued to use Excel to publish them. It was discovered that HTML files renamed with a suffix of XLS were read automatically as spreadsheets by Excel, and tables copied from the Web pages generated by SAS Enterprise Guide could be pasted successfully into existing Excel files too. This meant that, if the table could be created in a fixed layout and copied into a specific location, Excel formulas and macros could still be used to finish the reports.

At about the same time SAS Enterprise Guide 1.3 was installed on the PCs, SAS/GRAPH software was installed on the server, so that the users could incorporate their graphical reports into their SAS reporting. Somewhat surprisingly little use has been made of SAS/GRAPH, mainly because of their continuing and extensive use of Excel charts.

6.5.3 User Perception

Users of the SAS Enterprise Guide interface to the SAS data warehouse were asked the following questions approximately 18 months after its introduction. Their answers have been edited for clarity and to remove proprietary names.

Question 1: How would you compare SAS with the Visual Basic Application and SPSS for the processing and analysis of mainframe data?

User 1: SAS is much quicker and more flexible. Before, in the Visual Basic application, we had to output a lot of reports because we could only do crosstabulation with two variables.

User 2: SAS is far superior in terms of processing and analysis power. However, the point-and-click of the Visual Basic application is easier to learn.

Question 2: How would you compare SAS Enterprise Guide with Excel for analyzing and presenting the data to management?

User 1: Generally, SAS is better for analyzing data, although I use Excel for sorting smaller data sets because it is easier.

User 2: We still create all our reports and charts in Excel; we get the raw data from SAS and make it more presentable in Excel. For our standard reports and charts we have a consistent output from SAS that is linked in Excel to a more presentable output.

Question 3: Do you use the graphical parts of SAS Enterprise Guide, or just use Excel for the production of charts?

User 1: No, Excel seems better (i.e., double-axis graphs), and I am more familiar with it.

User 2: Excel only.

Question 4: Do the GUIs in SAS Enterprise Guide:

(a) help you on a day-to-day basis?

(b) help you when you forget the exact syntax of SAS procedures like PROC TABULATE?

(c) help you hardly at all now?

User 1: (c) No, I tend to copy old code instead.

User 2: (c) I hardly use it at all now; most of our output is PROC TABULATE. We usually manipulate an existing piece of code.

6.5.4 Conclusions

- SAS Enterprise Guide can be used instead of a locally installed SAS system to replace existing applications, provided there are obvious benefits, e.g., reducing the amount of data required to be transferred to and from the user's PC.

- It is important to introduce SAS/GRAPH with specific training as early as possible; otherwise, existing software used for producing graphs will continue to be used.

- SAS Enterprise Guide users do not need to use the GUIs to find SAS Enterprise Guide valuable.

6.5.5 What Happened Next

- At the time of writing this book, the client has been using SAS Enterprise Guide continuously for over four years.

- The client now has SAS Enterprise Guide 4.1 installed.

- The biggest problem experienced by the newer SAS Enterprise Guide users is caused by not realizing that the SAS programs are actually running on the UNIX server, and not on their PC. This causes confusion about where their input data must be located, and where their output is stored.

- The newer SAS Enterprise Guide users are using the GUIs to develop SAS programs, but the more experienced users are writing most of their SAS programs by copying and pasting from existing code.

6.6 Recommended Reading

For more information, go to
www.hollandnumerics.com/books/Saving_Time_and_Money_using_SAS.htm. This
page includes a chapter-by-chapter list of recommended reading.

Index

Books Available from SAS Press

Advanced Log-Linear Models Using SAS®
by **Daniel Zelterman**

Analysis of Clinical Trials Using SAS®: A Practical Guide
by **Alex Dmitrienko, Geert Molenberghs, Walter Offen,** and **Christy Chuang-Stein**

Annotate: Simply the Basics
by **Art Carpenter**

Applied Multivariate Statistics with SAS® Software, Second Edition
by **Ravindra Khattree** and **Dayanand N. Naik**

Applied Statistics and the SAS® Programming Language, Fifth Edition
by **Ronald P. Cody** and **Jeffrey K. Smith**

An Array of Challenges — Test Your SAS® Skills
by **Robert Virgile**

Building Web Applications with SAS/IntrNet®: A Guide to the Application Dispatcher
by **Don Henderson**

Carpenter's Complete Guide to the SAS® Macro Language, Second Edition
by **Art Carpenter**

Carpenter's Complete Guide to the SAS® REPORT Procedure
by **Art Carpenter**

The Cartoon Guide to Statistics
by **Larry Gonick** and **Woollcott Smith**

Categorical Data Analysis Using the SAS® System, Second Edition
by **Maura E. Stokes, Charles S. Davis,** and **Gary G. Koch**

Cody's Data Cleaning Techniques Using SAS® Software
by **Ron Cody**

Common Statistical Methods for Clinical Research with SAS® Examples, Second Edition
by **Glenn A. Walker**

The Complete Guide to SAS® Indexes
by **Michael A. Raithel**

CRM Segmemtation and Clustering Using SAS® Enterprise Miner™
by **Randall S. Collica**

Data Management and Reporting Made Easy with SAS® Learning Edition 2.0
by **Sunil K. Gupta**

Data Preparation for Analytics Using SAS®
by **Gerhard Svolba**

Debugging SAS® Programs: A Handbook of Tools and Techniques
by **Michele M. Burlew**

Decision Trees for Business Intelligence and Data Mining: Using SAS® Enterprise Miner™
by **Barry de Ville**

Efficiency: Improving the Performance of Your SAS® Applications
by **Robert Virgile**

The Essential Guide to SAS® Dates and Times
by **Derek P. Morgan**

Fixed Effects Regression Methods for Longitudinal Data Using SAS®
by **Paul D. Allison**

Genetic Analysis of Complex Traits Using SAS®
by **Arnold M. Saxton**

A Handbook of Statistical Analyses Using SAS®, Second Edition
by **B.S. Everitt**
and **G. Der**

Health Care Data and SAS®
by **Marge Scerbo, Craig Dickstein,**
and **Alan Wilson**

The How-To Book for SAS/GRAPH® Software
by **Thomas Miron**

In the Know... SAS® Tips and Techniques From Around the Globe, Second Edition
by **Phil Mason**

Instant ODS: Style Templates for the Output Delivery System
by **Bernadette Johnson**

Integrating Results through Meta-Analytic Review Using SAS® Software
by **Morgan C. Wang**
and **Brad J. Bushman**

Introduction to Data Mining Using SAS® Enterprise Miner™
by **Patricia B. Cerrito**

Learning SAS® by Example: A Programmer's Guide
by **Ron Cody**

Learning SAS® in the Computer Lab, Second Edition
by **Rebecca J. Elliott**

The Little SAS® Book: A Primer
by **Lora D. Delwiche**
and **Susan J. Slaughter**

The Little SAS® Book: A Primer, Second Edition
by **Lora D. Delwiche**
and **Susan J. Slaughter**
(updated to include SAS 7 features)

The Little SAS® Book: A Primer, Third Edition
by **Lora D. Delwiche**
and **Susan J. Slaughter**
(updated to include SAS 9.1 features)

The Little SAS® Book for Enterprise Guide® 3.0
by **Susan J. Slaughter**
and **Lora D. Delwiche**

The Little SAS® Book for Enterprise Guide® 4.1
by **Susan J. Slaughter**
and **Lora D. Delwiche**

Logistic Regression Using the SAS® System: Theory and Application
by **Paul D. Allison**

Longitudinal Data and SAS®: A Programmer's Guide
by **Ron Cody**

Maps Made Easy Using SAS®
by **Mike Zdeb**

Models for Discrete Date
by **Daniel Zelterman**

Multiple Comparisons and Multiple Tests Using SAS® Text and Workbook Set
(books in this set also sold separately)
by **Peter H. Westfall, Randall D. Tobias,**
Dror Rom, Russell D. Wolfinger,
and **Yosef Hochberg**

Multiple-Plot Displays: Simplified with Macros
by **Perry Watts**

Multivariate Data Reduction and Discrimination with SAS® Software
by **Ravindra Khattree**
and **Dayanand N. Naik**

Output Delivery System: The Basics
by **Lauren E. Haworth**

support.sas.com/pubs

Painless Windows: A Handbook for SAS® Users, Third Edition
by **Jodie Gilmore**
(updated to include SAS 8 and SAS 9.1 features)

Pharmaceutical Statistics Using SAS®: A Practical Guide
Edited by **Alex Dmitrienko, Christy Chuang-Stein, and Ralph D'Agostino**

The Power of PROC FORMAT
by **Jonas V. Bilenas**

PROC SQL: Beyond the Basics Using SAS®
by **Kirk Paul Lafler**

PROC TABULATE by Example
by **Lauren E. Haworth**

Professional SAS® Programmer's Pocket Reference, Fifth Edition
by **Rick Aster**

Professional SAS® Programming Shortcuts, Second Edition
by **Rick Aster**

Quick Results with SAS/GRAPH® Software
by **Arthur L. Carpenter and Charles E. Shipp**

Quick Results with the Output Delivery System
by **Sunil Gupta**

Reading External Data Files Using SAS®: Examples Handbook
by **Michele M. Burlew**

Regression and ANOVA: An Integrated Approach Using SAS® Software
by **Keith E. Muller and Bethel A. Fetterman**

SAS For Dummies®
by **Stephen McDaniel and Chris Hemedinger**

SAS® for Forecasting Time Series, Second Edition
by **John C. Brocklebank and David A. Dickey**

SAS® for Linear Models, Fourth Edition
by **Ramon C. Littell, Walter W. Stroup, and Rudolf Freund**

SAS® for Mixed Models, Second Edition
by **Ramon C. Littell, George A. Milliken, Walter W. Stroup, Russell D. Wolfinger, and Oliver Schabenberger**

SAS® for Monte Carlo Studies: A Guide for Quantitative Researchers
by **Xitao Fan, Ákos Felsővályi, Stephen A. Sivo, and Sean C. Keenan**

SAS® Functions by Example
by **Ron Cody**

SAS® Graphics for Java: Examples Using SAS® AppDev Studio™ and the Output Delivery System
by **Wendy Bohnenkamp and Jackie Iverson**

SAS® Guide to Report Writing, Second Edition
by **Michele M. Burlew**

SAS® Macro Programming Made Easy, Second Edition
by **Michele M. Burlew**

SAS® Programming by Example
by **Ron Cody and Ray Pass**

SAS® Programming for Researchers and Social Scientists, Second Edition
by **Paul E. Spector**

SAS® Programming in the Pharmaceutical Industry
by **Jack Shostak**

SAS® Survival Analysis Techniques for Medical Research, Second Edition
by **Alan B. Cantor**

SAS® System for Elementary Statistical Analysis, Second Edition
by **Sandra D. Schlotzhauer and Ramon C. Littell**

support.sas.com/pubs

SAS® System for Regression, Third Edition
by **Rudolf J. Freund**
and **Ramon C. Littell**

SAS® System for Statistical Graphics, First Edition
by **Michael Friendly**

The SAS® Workbook and Solutions Set
(books in this set also sold separately)
by **Ron Cody**

Selecting Statistical Techniques for Social Science Data: A Guide for SAS® Users
by **Frank M. Andrews, Laura Klem, Patrick M. O'Malley, Willard L. Rodgers, Kathleen B. Welch,**
and **Terrence N. Davidson**

Statistical Quality Control Using the SAS® System
by **Dennis W. King**

Statistics Using SAS® Enterprise Guide®
by **James B. Davis**

A Step-by-Step Approach to Using the SAS® System for Factor Analysis and Structural Equation Modeling
by **Larry Hatcher**

A Step-by-Step Approach to Using SAS® for Univariate and Multivariate Statistics, Second Edition
by **Norm O'Rourke, Larry Hatcher,**
and **Edward J. Stepanski**

Step-by-Step Basic Statistics Using SAS®: Student Guide and Exercises
(books in this set also sold separately)
by **Larry Hatcher**

Survival Analysis Using SAS®:
A Practical Guide
by **Paul D. Allison**

Tuning SAS® Applications in the OS/390 and z/OS Environments, Second Edition
by **Michael A. Raithel**

Univariate and Multivariate General Linear Models: Theory and Applications Using SAS® Software
by **Neil H. Timm**
and **Tammy A. Mieczkowski**

Using SAS® in Financial Research
by **Ekkehart Boehmer, John Paul Broussard,**
and **Juha-Pekka Kallunki**

Using the SAS® Windowing Environment:
A Quick Tutorial
by **Larry Hatcher**

Visualizing Categorical Data
by **Michael Friendly**

Web Development with SAS® by Example, Second Edition
by **Frederick E. Pratter**

Your Guide to Survey Research Using the SAS® System
by **Archer Gravely**

JMP® Books

Elementary Statistics Using JMP®
by **Sandra D. Schlotzhauer**

JMP® for Basic Univariate and Multivariate Statistics: A Step-by-Step Guide
by **Ann Lehman, Norm O'Rourke, Larry Hatcher,**
and **Edward J. Stepanski**

JMP® Start Statistics, Third Edition
by **John Sall, Ann Lehman,**
and **Lee Creighton**

Regression Using JMP®
by **Rudolf J. Freund, Ramon C. Littell,**
and **Lee Creighton**

support.sas.com/pubs